In Search of Honor

Lessons from Workers
on
How to Build Trust

Adele B. Lynn

Publisher's Cataloging-in-Publication
(Provided by Quality Books, Inc.)

Lynn, Adele B.
    In search of honor : lessons from workers on how to build trust and spark inspiration / Adele B. Lynn. — 1st ed.
    p.cm.
    Preassigned LCCN: 98-71506
    ISBN: 0-9664084-4-6
    1. Employee motivation. 2. Leadership. 3. Business ethics.   I. Title.

HF5549.5.M63L96 1998   658.3'14
                                        QBI98-675

Published by BajonHouse Publishing

TABLE OF CONTENTS

FOREWORD

LEADERSHIP IS A CALLING. To do it well, the leader must have a philosophy that guides and directs his or her actions. This book provides the leader with a philosophy. The collective wisdom of the everyday worker is the basis for this philosophy. The cumulative voices of nearly one thousand interviews with burly pipe fitters, pristine clerics, cynical professionals, and trapped supervisors and factory workers shout, what I consider, the truth about how to build honor and inspire people in the workplace.

In Part I of this book, extracted from the words of these workers, the secrets of building trust unfold. Trust is nothing more than a by-product of everyday actions between leader and follower. I have chosen to group these actions into four categories and chapters. They are: Importance, Touch, Gratitude, and Contributions.

Trust is the essential building block for any leader. Without it, there is no foundation, no launching pad, for anything else. The philosophy in this book calls for the leader to constantly build trust with each action, with each employee, each day.

Part II of this book explains the leader's essential role in providing vision in the workplace. With the organization's mission established, the leader's job of putting pictures to the mission and inviting workers to join in the dream begins. The leader's ability to keep the vision alive often determines the success or failure of the business.

Passion, persistence, and patience provide fuel to the vision on a daily basis.

A leader cannot lead until he or she knows him or herself. No philosophy can take hold in a soul that doesn't have depth and understanding. My intent isn't to shove this philosophy in your face and expect you to believe it.

Instead, I would like for you to reflect on the voices of the people who we interviewed and decide their truth. This section, Part III, asks leaders to contemplate some tough questions. Questions that are central to the philosophy espoused in this book.

Through this reflection, you are, of course, free to accept or reject all or part of this philosophy as your own. My hope is that by building a better understanding of your own soul, you will become more capable of understanding and reaching others.

In the final section, Part IV, I hope to plant a dream — a dream of sparking the fires of inspiration in the people whom you touch. If you keep this dream in your heart, I think the true mission of leadership stays focused.

To better hear the voices of everyday workers, I have included a collection of letters that appear at the end of each chapter. These letters summarize some of the feelings that employees harbor and these caustic, hilarious, and serious messages hit leaders in the gut. As you read, can you see yourself on any of the pages? If so, take the wisdom inside and reflect on a better way.

My dedication to the philosophy voiced on these pages deepened in two ways. Since 1982, I watched my clients lose trust with their workers and, I hope to think, I helped them gain it back. I watched them sometimes flounder without vision. I also watched as they focused the vision, added fuel and passion, and achieved brighter futures. I also watched many courageous individual leaders develop as they learned more about themselves — more about the core of their being that they called on for strength.

The second way that I became committed to this philosophy was through my own ignorance, mistakes, and failures. Through my own human frailties I learned what works and what doesn't work. I learned to build trust, because I lost trust. I learned to have vision, because I had no vision. I learned who I was, because I didn't know who I was.

The greatest rewards came as small surprises along the way. People whom I had touched and affirmed somewhere in time, probably by accident instead of design, came back to say thank you. They said I sometimes made a difference. Some were so generous as to say that I inspired them. I know that I did not, because I know that inspiration can only be sparked — the true fire comes from a Higher Source.

As workers search for honor, the leader who finds ways to give it freely, ultimately is the one who finds honor.

TRUST
COMES FIRST

INTRODUCTION

THE ELUSIVE FACTOR CALLED TRUST is something that every workplace needs and every leader or aspiring leader must know how to build. Any hope of inspired performance is shattered without this basic tenet.

Trust makes life easier. It's just less of a struggle when you don't have to worry about your credibility. When your integrity and everything you say or do as a leader is suspect, then much of your energy is spent defending yourself. Your creativity and focus drain away.

Leaders without high trust struggle through even the simplest changes. Hostility, challenge, and suspect become the norm. On the contrary, leaders who possess a high perception of trust can accomplish most anything.

So just what is this trust thing and how can you get it? Well, you can't just get it. You have to develop it over time. First, it takes a mindset of honor and integrity. Every action, deed, and thought, must be put to the test before it becomes reality. The test is an "honor and integrity filter" that serves as a screen for the high-trust leader.

Employees, however, can't see trust. They can't see if a leader has his "honor and integrity filter" in place. What they see and therefore base their judgments on is the leader's behavior. The employees we interviewed defined four elements characteristic of trust. These four elements are: 1) a sense of importance, directed at both the work and the people; 2) touch (no, not the physical kind but rather, genuinely caring and treating people like human equals despite status); 3) expressed, sincere gratitude; and 4) fair and equal contributions in the workplace.

The critical underlying qualities that must be present in all inter-actions with employees are honor and integrity. There is a fine line between trust and manipulation, and honor and integrity define that line. We can see the four elements listed above used in a negative way when honor and integrity are absent.

Sadly, of the 1000 people interviewed, we found a striking absence of the behaviors that could lead to improved trust:

- ❖ 61% said their bosses don't place much importance on them or their tasks.

- ❖ 57% said their leaders don't care about them as people.

- ❖ 88% said they do not receive enough acknowledgment for the work they do.

- ❖ 62% said the workload is unfair.

Although the overall leadership of the organization was impor-tant, the direct manager, supervisor, or team leader held the most important key to whether employees perceived trust in their work environments.

With trust in hand, leaders invite others into the dream and build successes — both financial and beyond.

——➤◆◄——

Every day for twenty years he came and he went.

He never missed a day. He did his job and he went home.

He came back the following day and he did his job again.

And then he went home again.

But did it matter to anyone? No one ever really said.

He supposed that it did, but maybe it didn't.

He felt like a guppy in a sea of work.

——➤◆◄——

1. IMPORTANCE

Attaching Importance to People and Task

Does it matter to anyone that Michelangelo went to work and painted the ceiling of the Sistine Chapel? Does it matter to anyone that one day Dr. Christiaan Barnard went to work and performed the first human heart transplant? Does it matter to anyone that Ann went to work and filled a customer order correctly and in time for shipment? Does it matter to anyone that Joe went to work and accurately recorded a customer transaction in a large financial institution?

Yes, it matters! Or at least it should. All of these people have made a difference. Each one has significantly contributed to the leader's vision for the organization. (More about vision in Chapter 5.) Each one's task had importance. Without the task and the individuals, a project would fail.

But surely, what Dr. Barnard did mattered more. Maybe, but this isn't about mattering more. It is about each person making a difference in his own way. It is about each person contributing to the total. As a leader it is extremely important that you value the task and the contribution that each person makes.

Janice was the cleaning person in a large financial institution. When asked whether or not her job was important, she instantly replied, "Oh, yes, it is extremely important. What I do or don't do can affect everyone who comes in here. [And everyone has to go to the john some time.] If people come in here and it is messy and dirty, then they figure that's the way they should work, too."

Her boss often told her how important her job was. On one occasion, he told her specifically that she contributed to bringing in a new customer because the customer commented on how clean and well kept the bathroom was. He told her how her job fit into the vision and explained that what she did each day really was a significant part of the company strategy. He used importance as a coaching tool.

Each of us wants to believe we make a difference. We want to believe the work we do each day is somehow recognized and significant to some larger purpose or vision. If a leader can connect with this need, then he has begun to elevate the significance of the person himself. This very connection waters the seeds of trust and deepens the bonds in the workplace. Attaching importance to a task says: *I care about what you do every day. I am happy that you are here to do it. It makes a difference. You make a difference.*

Most people want meaningful work. This was best illustrated by Fred, a young man in my neighborhood who is mentally retarded. Fred recently got a job at a local restaurant, where he brings out fresh dishes of food for a bountiful buffet. He beams from ear to ear as he proudly dons a chef's hat and white jacket and carefully places the food in its appropriate spot on the tables. When asked how he likes his job he says, "I really like it. I am important now."

Granted, in the perspective of total life and the significance of mankind, packing a shipment accurately and on time is inconsequential, but, so much of life is made of the little things. Therefore, attaching importance to these things somehow communicates a larger message: Each of us is important and connected to a larger, more significant picture in work and mankind. People who do not feel valued or significant in other aspects of their life need the importance that is attached to their work. It is the only thread of value their lives hold.

If you ignore the significance of your people's work, then how can you expect your employees to value the work they do? Your message of importance sets the tone for each detail to be carried through, for each task to be done with pride, and for each person to believe she has made a difference.

It is the leader's job to nurture the spirit of importance in the workplace. The leader's belief in the vision is the first statement saying what everyone does every day is worthwhile. After that, when the leader tells each person how he contributes to the vision, she says that what everyone does every day is important. This also helps set the expectation that each person will do his job right.

It is easy to get caught up in the argument that workers have lost their pride in workmanship — that people just don't care — that the work ethic has eroded to a critical point of apathy. But this type of discussion won't bring it back. You can blame parents, or schools, or society's values, and in doing so, sidestep your responsibility as leaders in the workplace and resign yourselves to accept this mediocrity. Or, as leaders, you can create a new environment in your workplace, an environment that will nurture and foster the best in all those whom you touch.

This environment says "slinging burgers here is an incredibly worthwhile endeavor."

Rosie said that one of the people who inspired her to do her very best was Katie, the manager of the local fast-food restaurant where she worked in high school. Rosie said that somehow Katie communicated that what she was doing was nearly as important as a moon launch. She instilled in Rosie the sense that every order of french fries Rosie filled was important. Also, Katie always talked about "the benefits of learning everything possible, even though this is just a temporary job in high school, because what you learn here will make you better equipped than others who don't have this wonderful opportunity." Rosie said that often on paydays, the kids used to tease Katie that maybe they owed her for the privilege of working there — and maybe they did. It is no wonder that this was no ordinary burger place. This franchise had received the highest honor, the "Gold Award," for the last four years — ever since Katie had become manager.

Attaching Importance to People

> *If you value the task over the person,*
> *the meaning of importance will be lost.*

As a leader, you must always keep in perspective that leadership requires balancing the importance of the people and the importance of the task. Too often, leaders with clear vision see precisely the tasks that can lead to the vision and they begin to push toward the task. There is nothing wrong with this, provided they don't lose sight of the fact that it is the people who will ultimately deliver the task.

The enlightened leader attaches importance to every person on her team. She demonstrates and communicates that all of them are needed to accomplish the vision and that they and they alone are best suited to do their job.

Unfortunately, the typical mode of operation is that when production numbers or quality numbers go south, the typical leader calls the troops together for a focus meeting on the numbers. The typical speech goes something like this:

"We have a real crisis here; our numbers are really low. You have to come through and realize how serious this is. We are in danger of not meeting our goals and if this happens, we may not have a job. Corporate could shut us down without blinking an eye."

Well, that is all well and good and most probably true. It certainly attaches importance to the task, and that is necessary. But the tone of this message and most similar messages, is that they don't value the individuals who are coming to work each day. Perhaps another approach would first value and make significant the people themselves:

"Look, I believe that no one can build a better widget than each of you. Over the years, you have proven this over and over again. We have been in some serious situations in the past and you have always come through. Unfortunately, we are in a major crunch right now — we are seriously behind in meeting our production goal. What kinds of things have you done in the past or new things could be done that could help get us out of this mess? No one can do it except you, and I don't believe anyone can do it better. I am here to answer questions or give you any information you need. I am also here to listen to what you have to say about this problem and its solution. How shall we begin?"

The tone of all the messages that we give is the "importance scale" that our team is reading. If the tone shows disgust or discouragement with the situation, the team picks up the message that the leader is disgusted or discouraged with them. If the tone is that this task isn't very important or that other tasks are so much more important, then the team reads that they are somehow less important. Over and over again, all day long, you are communicating both the importance of the task and the importance of your team members. Team members are constantly reading your nonverbal signals, your priorities, and your attention to determine where they and their tasks fit on the importance scale.

Attaching significance and importance to the people cannot be an after-thought. People will know if it is. As a leader you must set this goal for yourself and work to meet it. Each message, each day, must contain the elements of significance. At first, perhaps, you will need to plan this important message. But after a while, it should be so ingrained in your philosophy that you will deliver it naturally and regularly to your team.

In concert with attaching importance to your people is a mindset that places you at the bottom of your team — not at the top. You work for your team members, helping them to get the job done. You are there to run interference, to gather information, or to otherwise support and assist the team. If you recognize your place in this inverted hierarchy, your team becomes your customer. You must serve your team with the same zeal with which you would expect them to serve the customer. There isn't much room for forgotten promises or lack of followup or an attitude that says, "I'm too busy right now."

Pam had been promoted to front-line manager. She devoted much of her day to getting paperwork and schedules together. Between the paperwork and the meetings she had to attend, she had little time for anything else. Over time, her area deteriorated – problems grew, production and quality suffered. People in the area complained that Pam was always too busy and couldn't be bothered with them. They received the message that they and their tasks lacked importance – not at all the message Pam intended, but indeed, the message her team received.

But shouldn't we expect people to take care of their own problems and think ahead and perform their jobs? Yes, we should. But it's the leader who must take steps to empower the team, first by fostering a sense of importance in the individuals who make up the team. The leader must firmly believe three things:

1) The tasks that his team is working on are important.

2) Each member of the team is important.

3) The leader is there to serve the team.

These three elements are the very roots of empowerment. If as a leader, you don't believe these three things, then either get rid of the task because it isn't contributing to the vision, get a new team or team member, or seriously adjust your thinking about leadership.

Of all the people I talked with, my most lasting impression comes from Daisy. She told me about dignity, a word I hadn't used in concert with importance, but that obviously has profound meaning.

> You could tell from looking at her face that she understood the meaning of "dignity." She carried herself in a way that suggested importance. Her head was high and her eyes clear.
>
> It was also apparent that she had known a gut full of indignities, each leaving a mark on her soul, but never truly dimming her spirit. Her voice was firm and somewhat angry when she spoke about the way management had done things in the past.

"They just told you. They didn't bother to ask. They didn't care. You didn't have a choice. They were the boss, and they let you know in no uncertain terms."

Recently, a severe computer failure had rendered an entire day of processing unusable. The entire reconciling operation was in chaos and much of the work had to be reconstructed by hand. This disaster would take weeks if not months to correct. Management needed the employees' help to resolve the situation, and it knew it. Management asked the employees for their assistance.

Her face and her voice softened when she spoke of "this time."

"What was different Daisy?" I asked.

"This time," Daisy said, "they did it with dignity."

"I still don't understand, Daisy," I said. "Can you tell me more?"

"They treated us as if we were important," she said. "They told us that they needed us and that they really needed our help. They *asked* us if we would please stay to help with this work. They explained why it was so important and that they couldn't do it without us. They said they understood if we had other commitments that would prevent us from staying, and we were told that they wouldn't hold it against us. They gave us a choice — and we came through. It was about respect — on both sides. It was good. Dignity. It was with dignity."

"And how did it feel to be honored like that?" I asked.

"You can't describe honor and dignity. You can only feel it." Daisy said. "You just know. It comes from their heart."

Spirit Killers and Soul Suckers

CELEBRITY EGO

It is hard, if not impossible, to attach importance to another person or to someone else's task if we can't get the focus off of ourselves. If we see the world as an extension of ourselves, then, we're going to have a difficult time honoring anyone else with a sense of importance. Or if everyone else's place has to be secondary to our own, the sense of importance will be diluted and false.

Know your place as a leader. If you humble yourself to your team, your sense of importance will be heightened and your team's will skyrocket.

MISPLACED CREDIT

If you can't deflect the credit for a job well done away from yourself and back to your team, then you don't understand the concept of attaching importance to others.

As harmful as taking the credit yourself is misplaced credit. As a leader, it is important that you know who does what — individuals seek credit and importance, and it is your job as a leader to make sure those who deserve it get it. Nothing can be so demoralizing as having worked your butt off on a project and watching someone who didn't contribute walk away with all the credit. Although this may have happened to you, you need to be sure that this doesn't happen to the people you lead.

John, a senior designer, told about a time when he was working on a complicated design of a piece of glassware. He worked with a young engineer, Dennis, who was competent, but also self-centered. A particular angle was giving them a real challenge, and the molds they were using were just not producing the desired effect. One day, John came in with an approach that completely changed the concept of the mold design they had been using. It worked! John was pleased and proud of what he had done. The division manager was visiting the plant one day shortly after the design had been put into manufacturing. John's boss introduced Dennis as the young engineer who had worked on the successful design — and failed to mention John's efforts. It was true, Dennis had worked on the design, but his was more of a support role. John had conceived the design.

John was crushed on two counts. First, his boss didn't even mention his efforts. Apparently he didn't even realize what John had contributed. Second, Dennis didn't bother to correct the perception that he had done all the work. John's sense of importance in the eyes of others was diminished.

But why should it matter? John knew the truth.

Yes, but it's nice to believe that others know the truth as well.

Dear Boss,

You never cease to amaze me! How could anyone have such an exalted opinion of herself? Is this what you learned in your MBA classes?

Haven't you figured out that I am an adult? I actually function all evening and weekend without being supervised! You have never given me the benefit of believing that I have a brain. You think that brains only exist if you have a title of supervisor or above. Well, OK. I will live up to your expectations. Every day I will come to work and make sure I leave my brain at home. I will wait until you tell me what to do. I will do only what I am told. I will let you do all the thinking. I'll save my brain for the evenings and weekends.

I find you to be so insulting, but I also find you to be amusing. I shake my head in amazement and think to myself, "You smart fool. If you would only ask. I've been doing this for 20 years. I just might know something about this."

Enjoy yourself now because you're going to burn out. Unfortunately, you bring out the worst in me. I hope you do burn out and go away.

Dear Boss,

The name is Josephine E. Gidy. I have worked here for 23 years. I cleaned your office when you worked on the 3rd floor in accounting. I also cleaned it when you worked on the 12th floor in the operations department. Now that you occupy the big suite as we call it, I clean it still.

I pass you every single morning on my way out. Sometimes you say hello. Most of the time you don't even bother to make eye contact with me. You have never once called me by my name. It's as though I am invisible.

Oh, once about 6 years ago you did speak to me. I had hurt my back and couldn't clean as well under the desk as I should. You told me that there was some paper that I had forgotten to pick up and that it's been there for over a week.

Thanks boss, it was nice chatting with you that day.

Sincerely,
Josephine E. Gidy

"You are worthwhile.

You are worth my time and effort.

You make a difference

in this workplace and in this world.

I care about you as a person."

2. TOUCH

Genuine Caring

The rare leaders, who deliver this message to the people they lead, know how to connect with and inspire people. They know how to touch.

Before the sexual harassment attorneys start preparing their briefs, let's make it clear that we are in no way referring to or suggesting physical touch. Instead, we are talking about the immense power to touch with words that honor the spirit of another human being. These words could be as simple as "Good Morning," but they must be delivered with enough warmth and genuineness so that the person who receives the "touch" instantly feels the power.

As a leader, it is your responsibility to find the touch that opens your employees' hearts.

Before you can find the right touch, you must know who your employees are. What are they all about? What is important to them? Do they have any hobbies, outside interests? Do they have any worries? Burdens? Crises?

I used to accompany a leader of a large coal mine on many trips through the mines and in the outside areas where his coal-smudged people were hard at work. I soon learned that it was never a quick walk to our destination. He always stopped to talk with people. Sometimes he talked about production problems, sometimes he talked about the upcoming shipment and why it was so important. But just as often, the conversation revolved around personal matters: How was this child doing or that mother? Did they get their test results back from the doctor's visit? Are they feeling better now? Did they get that new car they were looking at? Has that leak been taken care of? Did they catch any salmon this year? What kind of bait were they using? On and on the mini conversations flowed — connecting him with each person on a special level.

The other thing I noticed was this man's facial expressions — always appropriate for the conversation. You could feel the "real" coming from his soul. So could his workers. The result of these mini-conversations? In a four-year effort, the mine had recovered from a $45-million dollar loss to a $25-million dollar profit.

I'm not naive enough to attribute this kind of turnaround solely to mini-conversations this dynamic leader initiated. Some wise business decisions were made here as well. But after witnessing this constant genuine display of caring and warmth, I found a magical connection between this leader and his people. In no way am I insinuating that everyone was "on board." Some people suspected his friendliness. As time went on, a few die-hard skeptics remained, but more and more people accepted this man as genuine.

Touch can't be relegated to a program. It can't be monitored and tracked for results. Models can't be created and words can't be crafted so that the manager knows exactly what to say. You see, touch isn't an exact kind of expression. It is an art form. It is custom tailored to the individual, expressly crafted by the individual who is doing the touching. There are no patterns or molds, and each touch must be specifically crafted. You may argue, then, that this could be time consuming. After all, we all know that in our pre-fab world we don't have time for hand-crafting. However, I suggest that it takes very little time compared to the impact it delivers. How many hours and dollars does your employer spend on recognition or reward programs that seem to have little or no impact? Touch doesn't cost money. It just takes a leader who devotes some time to know what opens the hearts of his employees. Then and only then are you capable of the magic of touch.

Using Touch to Nurture Workplace Spirit

Have you ever walked into a place and been able to feel the atmosphere? If you pay attention, you can tell if it is stressed or creative or pleasant or chaotic. Each workplace has an individual and distinctive spirit.

It is the leader who sets the tone for the spirit in the workplace. The leader composes and directs the melody of corporate life, and the workers dance to whatever tune is played. The dance is dictated by the music itself. The leader chooses the rhythm and the tune — from funeral march to a joyful waltz. Listen to your workplace: What kind of music is playing?

The most dramatic way to influence the spirit in the workplace is through touch. How you interact with your employees day after day has the greatest impact on the spirit, and it is through touch that you awaken the spirit. If you pay attention to this one aspect of leadership, you can dramatically change the tune of your workplace. Remember, each and every day you send touch messages that are translated into spirit. As a leader, wouldn't you rather take control of the spirit that prevails? The astute leader realizes the need to manage the "touch" as well as the budget.

> Donna manages a project-oriented operation with about 40 people. Her frequent travels take her out of the office for several days or even weeks at a time. She had a project-team review meeting scheduled for her first day back in the office after an absence of nearly three weeks. She wanted to raise questions and concerns about a number of pressing projects. She figured those questions and concerns would require lots of immediate action. So, Donna wanted to get to the items quickly and get things moving, but she knew that if she came in with that approach, she would lose an opportunity to renew and refresh the workplace spirit. She decided instead to surprise her staff with breakfast rolls and coffee. She opened the meeting with:
>
> "I'm glad to be back. I missed you guys. How's

everyone?" Donna and her staff laughed together about George getting stuck in the mud at one of their remote client locations. Donna got an update on the bad weather she had missed on Monday and the ensuing two-hour traffic jam. She also heard about Pat's new puppy who "had an accident" on her new family room carpeting. After about 20 minutes of catching up on the office news, she revved up the pace, and her staff flew through the agenda. They did a lot of important work that day.

Nurturing the workplace spirit is a conscious choice. For some leaders, this may be a natural choice. For others, it requires a genuine effort by the leader. Developing a positive spirit in the workplace requires three fundamental ingredients:

❖ An attentive, genuine, active listening posture.

❖ Patience and tolerance for mistakes, fostering a no-blame culture.

❖ A belief that your people will come through.

If these three elements are in place, you can nurture spirit to new and improved heights.

The Listening Leader

Listening, truly listening, to the words, as well as to the underlying emotion is central to leadership that touches. Simply: If people don't think they are being listened to, they feel ignored. Ignored turns into neglected, neglected turns into angry, angry into apathetic, apathetic into empty. The workers become bodies that just go through the motions. Listening is foremost in developing bonds between leader and team member. You can make many mistakes, but as long as you are still listening, you are probably able to redeem your leadership to an acceptable level of performance.

I remember specifically asking an employee if she were ever inspired by any supervisor or leader where she worked. Jean quickly met my question with scorn.

"Are you kidding?" she said. "Management around here treats you like you don't even exist." She said that two years earlier, she had caught her fingers in a press. *While her fingers were still stuck in the press,* her supervisor approached and complained that her machine was turned off. She told him that her hand was stuck in the press. He didn't even look. He snapped back, "I'm tired of excuses around here. Get the damn machine running."

As it turned out, her little finger was broken and her ring finger was badly smashed. Jean's bitterness came through loudly when she summed it up. "He didn't even bother to listen to me."

Listening is powerful. Listening is confirming. It is a way to touch that takes little effort on the part of the leader, but the impact can be long lasting. In another interview, I heard about a very special person who took the time to listen.

John told me that 17 years ago he worked for a man who really inspired him. He said he could remember a single moment that made the difference. John's daughter had been sick and John nervously approached his new boss about needing some time off to travel with his daughter to an out-of-state hospital for some experimental medical treatment. He walked into his boss's office, and before he could say a word, his boss said to him, "John, you look upset. Is something wrong?" As John told him about the medical problems his daughter was having, his boss listened sympathetically. Again, before John asked about taking time off, his boss said, "You know, John, if you need some time off, or if medical expenses are not covered by our policy, you need to let me know." John broke down and cried in front of this man he barely knew. He had never expected that kind of response. He said afterward that he promised himself that on a daily basis, he would do whatever he could to try to anticipate and listen to the boss's needs at work, just as his boss had anticipated and listened to the needs of his heart at this critical moment in his life.

The cost of listening is small, yet at times, the cost savings can be enormous. Another story that I found linked listening, cost savings, and inspiration in one neat package.

I was interviewing three members of a work team in an organization that had recently implemented a TQM effort to improve quality. This work team was asked to recommend ways to improve quality and productivity in its work area. As the team members told their story, they became more and more excited. The team members said that for years there had been a problem with backlog at the end of the month in their production cycle. Several of the employees had told management that they could reduce the backlog if they changed the work schedule to a four-day work week. Management was skeptical of the motives of the four-day work week and always rejected the idea.

Now, as a newly created work team, the members came to management with the same proposal. This time, Ned, the manager of the unit said, "You know, for years, I never listened to you when you suggested this. I still don't think it is a good idea, but if you are all in agreement that this is the right thing to do, I don't want to stand in the way. However, you guys need to show me that this really works over a long period of time."

The team implemented the four-day work week and Ned waited for the numbers. Week one productivity was down by four percent; week two productivity was down five percent; week three productivity was down two percent. Ned called a team meeting to discuss productivity. The team expected Ned to scrap the idea. However, Ned listened carefully when the team members explained why the productivity numbers had dropped and what steps they were taking to correct the problem. Ned asked the team if they needed anything from him to meet the goal. The team discussed a problem they were having with supplies, and Ned promised to look into it. Week four productivity numbers were even with the production figures before the schedule change. Week five posted a one percent gain in productivity. Week six posted another one percent gain. After a full year, the team was able not only to solve the end of month backlog problem, but overall the net gain in productivity was six percent, resulting in a $1.2-million cost savings. I was privileged to attend the one-year anniversary celebration party Ned had planned for the team. As Ned praised the team's contributions, he also apologized to the employees and also to his company for not listening sooner.

Patience and Tolerance — Creating a No-Blame Culture

Patience and tolerance for mistakes are also important qualities a leader must have in order to nurture workplace spirit. Most people aren't perfect yet; many of our systems and processes aren't perfect yet either. Therefore, mistakes will occur.

As a child, I worked in my family's grocery store. In those days, my parents delivered groceries for many of their customers. I remember when I was about 10 years old, I decided to help my dad load the station wagon for his evening deliveries. As my arms struggled to reach around the circumference of a large watermelon that was part of a customer's order, I heard my dad saying, "Be careful, that's a pretty big load." Of course it was, but then I was a big person, too. I made it to the middle of the paved parking lot in front of the store when my arms gave out. Splat! Watermelon everywhere. As my dad came to the rescue with a large broom and a box, to my surprise, he asked if I would go inside and get another watermelon and load it into the station wagon. Dad knew he needed to be tolerant of my error. He also knew by the tears in my eyes that my spirit was badly damaged. He also knew that the best cure was my own success.

Of course, it is important to manage errors and recurring problems and take steps to prevent problems. I am not suggesting that you lower your standards and accept more errors. Instead, set even higher standards, but find the cause for errors and work to eliminate them rather than place blame and demand that no errors are made. This no-blame culture is essential if you want to work toward inspiration points — those moments when the lights come on. Inspiration doesn't come without risk, and people will not take risk if they fear blame. Work toward no-blame, but insist your staff take responsibility for their errors and for correcting them with the leader's help.

No-blame says: "I tried something, it didn't work, I've made a mistake. I've created a problem. I will work to fix it," or even, "I need help to fix this." Here, the leader enables the fix. He finds or helps the staff to find the cause, determines if something may be salvaged, and moves forward.

No accountability says: "I don't care if it's my job, I'm not going to do it. Who cares? It doesn't matter." Here, the leader quickly focuses accountability and says: "Oh yes it does matter, and I care, and you need to care, also." Patience and tolerance for mistakes in no way imply that we lower our standards or that we drop accountability. In fact, no-blame will enable us to raise our standards and heighten our accountability.

A particular plant that I worked in had a tyrannical leader whose reputation for firing people was known throughout the company. Everyone lived in fear of this man's rage. Managers and employees alike spent their energy hiding mistakes from this tyrant. Managers, in fact, would lie to protect employees and employees would lie to protect the managers. As you would expect, however, this kind of atmosphere failed to uncover mistakes and work toward continuous improvement. No one wanted to admit mistakes for fear people would be punished or even fired. Therefore, the plant was plagued with recurring problems and inefficient systems.

A new leader, Ross, replaced the tyrant. He was dedicated to continuous improvement and strongly encouraged a no-blame attitude. Soon after Ross arrived, he began to ask questions pointing to potential problems in production. People did what they always did — they covered up, minimized and lied to the new leader about the problems. Eventually, Ross saw the pattern and decided that he had to take some drastic steps to change this or the plant would not survive.

He called a meeting of all employees. He explained that he knew that people had not been honest with him about problems. He cited several examples. Then, he made an announcement that sounded more like it was coming from the old tyrant. He wanted everyone to know and consider themselves forewarned that anyone who lied, misrepresented a problem, or withheld information from him regarding a problem, would be fired.

Within a week, Ross had learned that a manager had misrepresented a problem. Ross fired him immediately — no discussions, no written warning, no coaching.

Why such an act from a person who truly believed in a no-blame approach to problems? Wasn't this a contradiction? As Ross discussed his actions with me, he explained that he believed that it would have taken years of coaching to gain the no-blame culture that he desired. He viewed withholding information or misrepresenting problems as the single most destructive issue facing the plant. From that point on, the people in that plant knew the expectation. They knew that anything less than open discussion about problems could be grounds for dismissal.

Their fear didn't go away overnight. It took two years before people began to feel safe in telling the truth. During those two years, every time a person spoke the truth Ross said, "Thank you. I appreciate your honesty regarding this problem. Now we can focus on fixing it."

Within three years of Ross's leadership, the plant's productivity had improved by more than 13 percent. However, the intangible gains were summed up by a production worker named Alex who said, "It is so much easier to come to work now."

Believing in Your Team

The third element necessary for nurturing the spirit is a belief that your people will come through. When the leader believes and has a positive vision of her team, she contributes a powerful image that enables the team to do their jobs.

In order to deliver this kind of touch, the heart and soul of the leader must genuinely believe and want to honor another human being. The philosophy of the leader must be to regard his team members in such high esteem that he considers it a privilege to lead them. When the leader can feel that kind of intensity for his team, only then can he place honor at their feet.

One of the most incredible leaders that I have ever met is the president of a local glass conductor plant. Jim was talking one day to his management team about some of the problems gaining market share and competing in a world market where his off-shore competitors could produce the same product for pennies compared to his prices. He talked about how some of his team lacked experience and even education, for some of them had come up through the ranks.

Then he paused and said, "But this group of people, is the most wonderful and caring group I have ever imagined knowing in my lifetime. If anyone can deliver for me, these people can."

Jim was speaking from his heart. He envisioned these people as superstars. So, the employees who worked for this man believed they were special. He honored them in ways that no other leader had ever honored them — through his belief in them. In return, they were not just good performers for him, they were inspired. They reached inspiration points because Jim touched them in profound ways.

People respond to touch. People told me that the best leaders were the ones who cared about them. One of the issues that caught my attention in a series of special interviews was "turnaround" cases. I was curious when the performance of certain individuals appeared to change dramatically — for better or worse. In these instances, I was trying to determine how the leaders were different. Again, I heard the story of touch. People who thought the boss supported them were more likely to be named as good performers than people who thought their boss was adversarial. Yet, these were "turnaround" cases — not consistently good performers or consistently bad performers. The only difference we could determine was the perception the boss had of these employees.

> Abby was a front-line supervisor who worked for a
> manager who just did not believe she could come through
> and do the job. The manager admitted that she was intel-
> ligent and probably had the skill to do the job, but thought
> she just couldn't stay focused. He was convinced that she
> just wouldn't cut it, and to no one's surprise, he found
> fault after fault, thereby "proving" his point. Shortly there-
> after, this manager left the company, and Abby had a new
> boss. This boss had a vision that Abby would succeed,
> that Abby would be his best supervisor. In a matter of six
> months, lo and behold, Abby became a superstar. What
> really happened here? Did Abby's performance radically
> improve? Were the expectations of the second manager
> so much less? Or had Abby responded to the vision that
> each manager had for her?

In the short run, nurturing the workplace spirit may not significantly influence productivity, but in the interviews I conducted
regarding inspiration points, workers talked about how they would
do anything for certain leaders — leaders who had taken the time to
care. I heard some amazing stories of employees going beyond expectations because of an intense commitment to these leaders. What I

found was depth — depth that was reflected in productivity, creativity, and loyalty.

A more personal example of the power of touch came from an employee who spoke with deep respect and reverence about a supervisor who had changed her life.

"I don't know why you want to talk to me," she said. Janet's doe eyes quickly darted from my direct contact. She didn't know what to say.

"Rene Nichols told me that you are a terrific employee who has overcome many obstacles." I said.

"Rene helped me a lot." Carefully and slowly Janet told her story. "People told me I was a loser, and I guess I was," she said. "Rene was going to fire me. I had missed so many days. I just didn't come to work. I wanted to party, so I did. We have this policy where you get warnings if you miss too many days. I was on my final warning. Rene called me in and gave me the warning. It was real formal, in writing, and she was very stuffy. I just couldn't wait to get out of that office. Then, she said something to me that I will never forget."

Now Janet looked directly at me.

"She said, 'Janet, I see a very special person before me. Why are you trying so desperately to destroy her?'

"No one before ever said I was special. They all said I was a loser.

"I broke down and started to cry. I told Rene that I

had some problems. Rene said that if I really wanted help, I could get it. She said having problems isn't a crime, but not getting help is unexcusable. She gave me a number to call if I wanted some help. I called.

"But Rene didn't let me off the hook or use my problems as an excuse. She made it clear that I was still on final warning and that she would definitely fire me if I had an absence within so many days according to the policy. Then, she said that she would help me in any way she could.

"That was five years ago. If it wasn't for Rene, I am afraid to think what would have happened to me. It hasn't been easy or perfect. But I really changed.

"She has helped me in many other ways too. She suggested that I go back to school. I had just barely finished high school, and my grades were terrible. She told me about some remedial classes, and after about a year I got the courage to enroll at the local community college. I'm still going to school. I've also been promoted to another department. My life is on a totally different track than it was five years ago."

Just then, Rene entered the room where Janet and I had been talking. I asked Rene to tell me just what qualities she saw in Janet. Why didn't she just fire her and let it go?

"Although Janet had terrible attendance, when Janet did come to work, she was always willing to pitch in. She worked hard and she caught on quickly. Other people liked her, and she had a very special knack of drawing others into the work. I thought that if I could only reach her, touch her in some way, just maybe I could make a difference. Too many times I've tried with others, and you get no response. I was feeling rather hardened and cynical, and along came Janet. It was easy for me. I'm not the hero here. She is the one who did the work."

Touching the spirit of another human being in a positive and uplifting way can be one of the most rewarding things a leader can do. In the story of Janet and Rene, we can clearly see how Janet benefited, but as we spoke with Rene, we saw a leader who had emerged with a refreshed spirit. By overcoming her cynicism and using the power of touch, she inspired not only Janet, but also herself.

Touch isn't rote. It doesn't come from a textbook. You can't print it on little cards you carry in your shirt pocket. Touch can come only from the heart. It is touch — and touch alone — that transforms performance that is good into performance that is inspired. Inspiration comes from the soul. Only when the soul is stirred can it unleash the greatest achievements.

But the skeptics are saying this is ridiculous. You are lucky if you can get people to show up, let alone give inspiring performance — besides, how can a janitor be inspired?

When you walk into the bathroom that Wally cleaned, there is a difference. The sink bowls sparkle, you can see your reflection shining on the spotless floors, and the details are perfect: soap dispenser full, towel holders just right, and a fresh, clean scent in the air.

But what is really different? Why is it so much different from the restroom on the third floor, which Joe does every day? Talk to Wally and you will begin to understand. Talk to Joe and everything is confirmed.

Wally radiates spirit. He laughs, he smiles, he talks about his children and his family with a sense of pride. It's the same sense of pride you hear when he talks about his job — about "his" bathroom. When you talk with Joe, he complains constantly about his lot, he looks at his work with a very negative eye, he views the company in the same light.

Wally thinks his boss is the most caring and wonderful person alive. He told me that his boss is helping him with his General Educational Development certificate. Wally's mother is dying of cancer, and his boss asks about her every day. He said he would do anything for this man.

Joe, on the other hand, has a very different story and a very different boss. He said that the only time his boss ever talks to him is when he needs something or when he has a complaint. Otherwise, he says, he never sees him.

Many of you will argue that the difference lies in the hearts and souls of Wally and Joe instead of in their bosses. Perhaps Wally is just one of those intrinsically motivated individuals who would perform as well for anyone. Perhaps. But nearly everyone we spoke to who felt inspired at work attributed at least part of her inspiration to a leader "they would do anything for." Although it wasn't easy to find people who felt inspired at work, when we did, we heard about a leader who really cared about them as individuals. They spoke about their leaders' high expectations in one breath and their caring in the next — always connected.

Spirit Killer and Soul Suckers

BLAME

It's your fault. Why did you do something so stupid? How could you be so shortsighted? Why didn't you realize the impact of what you were doing? Why would you do something like that? Didn't you realize what was going to happen?

Not inquiry, blame. The difference is in the delivery. If I deliver it with judgment and ridicule, with just the right non-verbals, I have successfully blamed. Sophisticated blamers are very subtle. You have to listen carefully, but if you do, you will find all the elements of blame. Of course, the sophisticated blamer tells you the reason he is discussing this with you is that he wants you to learn from your mistakes. The aim of blame however, is shame. The blamer wants to help you realize just how stupid you are so that you can hide your head or wear a scarlet letter for the rest of your career. If you've ever been on the receiving end, you know exactly how this feels. You have certainly experienced the power of touch — negative touch.

We're not suggesting that as a leader you shouldn't confront performance issues — on the contrary, you must. It is the delivery and tone of those confrontations I am attacking. Blame serves no purpose. Time and time again, the reaction that is most often provoked by blame is denial, or embarrassment, or shame. If your aim is to inspire others to change their performance, they must be willing to accept and ultimately believe in what you have to say. You just can't get there from blame.

BEING TECHNIQUED

Phony. People see through it and they just don't like it. If any leader attempts to use this information as a technique to see if it works and he doesn't believe in it or deliver it from the heart, it won't work. This is not a technique, it is a philosophy. If you don't believe that it is the right thing to do, then you can't do it effectively. Even when you believe that it is the right thing to do, it will take some practice to make it feel smooth and unrehearsed. There are no 1, 2, 3, steps here to lead you through. You have to develop your own natural interpretation of what is presented here. If I present steps, I fear you will deliver steps — and not heart — and your people will see right though you.

Dear Manager,

The best in class for belittling is awarded to you! You have taken the art of belittling to new levels. You have excelled. Your continuous improvement efforts in this area are beyond reach.

I'd like to cite some specific examples of your outstanding work in this area.

- When Jill asked a question at the staff meeting and you responded with, "Duh...." This was brilliant belittling. It was done in front of all of us and it so nicely reinforced your consistent opinion of us.
- When Harry came in with a customer complaint and you told him to "Get your ass out of my office and into your chair and solve it." That was excellent advice and great belittling!
- When you told us we couldn't change our work schedules because you didn't trust we would do our job during the off hours without supervisors.

These few examples occurring just this week speak to your mastery of this skill. I guess the company will be asking you to train the new supervisors. After all, they might as well get it from the best.

Dear Manager,

You don't listen. And when you talk to us, you aren't open.

I wish you would treat us like adults. You treat us like children. You talk at us, not with us. You tell us what you think we should hear. You carefully weigh what you think we can handle. What is the big secret? It isn't fair to us. Besides, if we know what's going on, we can make better decisions. Maybe we can even help. We can handle the truth. Even if it's bad news, we would rather hear it straight than have you surprise us. In the end, lying to us isn't going to protect us. It will only cause us to distrust you.

It's maddening. You are so guarded. Even on the light side, you won't be open. Think about it. You won't even come out of your office and walk through the department.

I think you might have forgotten an important word. We are HUMAN resources. Treat us like human beings. Talk to us -- not at us -- and listen to us. Be honest.

"We just hear about it

when we do something wrong.

No one ever says anything

when we do something right.

Nobody ever says

thank you around here."

3. GRATITUDE

Cultivating an Attitude
of Gratitude

So what? Aren't we above such things? Who needs to hear such affirmations of gratitude? Why should we have to thank people for doing their job? That's what we pay people for — to do their jobs. Isn't that enough?

For a few, perhaps it is enough, but for a significant number of people, well-placed genuine gratitude builds good relationships. This special element of touch has a specific purpose. It honors the other person by acknowledging his effort, attitude, skill, or experience.

In the much-touted study done by Glenn Tobe and Associates, employees were asked to rank the importance of ten motivation factors. Likewise, supervisors were asked to rank the importance of the same ten factors for their employees.

The first three items, all dealing with the relationship side of leadership, were remarkably opposite. All the things employees said they wanted most were perceived as the least valued when the supervisors ranked the items. You'll also notice that "appreciation" topped the list.

Employees	Supervisors
Appreciation	Good wages
Feeling "in" on things	Job security
Understanding attitude	Promotion opportunities
Job security	Good working conditions
Good wages	Interesting work
Interesting work	Loyalty from management
Promotion opportunities	Tactful discipline
Loyalty from management	Appreciation
Good working conditions	Understanding attitude
Tactful discipline	Feeling "in" on things

Another interesting statistic comes from the U.S. Department of Labor. In 1995, it reported that 46 percent of people who quit their jobs did so because they felt unappreciated.

So this quality called appreciation must be very difficult, or quite expensive, or consume inordinate amounts of time, or surely it would abound in the workplace. Paradoxically, it is none of these things. It is very easy to do. It is absolutely free. It takes only a moment, yet it is perceived to be quite rare.

Brandon remembers his first job. Fresh from college and hired by a major company as a financial analyst, he was eager to please and ready for the challenge. When he was hired, he was told that a performance review would follow a six-month probation period. For the next six months, he was given numerous assignments and he worked diligently to complete them. However, during the six-month period, no one uttered a word about his performance. He started to worry around month three. He assumed that his performance must have been unacceptable because not one person had given him even a glimmer of hope or encouragement.

He remembers walking into his boss's office for his six-month review. He remembers the stone-faced look on his boss's face. As Brandon nervously shuffled some papers in a manilla folder, he distinctly remembered he prepared himself to be fired. The boss delivered the appraisal without showing any emotion. Brandon soon realized the boss was praising him. The appraisal ended with his boss saying, "Brandon, we are grateful for the good work that you have done, especially on the Pegasus project."

Brandon was stunned. He told his boss that he was surprised and that he was expecting to be fired because he hadn't heard anything positive. His boss said that the rule of thumb around the company was that if you didn't hear anything, consider it good news. He said that the company doesn't believe in going around thanking people for doing their jobs. If he was going to be a part of the team, he'd have to get used to it.

We heard similar stories in many companies. These stories confirmed that gratitude is in short supply. However, in another example, we find the power of this simple gift.

Barry contrasts his first five years at a particular company with the last two years. The difference? "My attitude is so much different now. I care about this place, I care about coming to work because my supervisor has the decency to say thank you."

Barry told us that for five years he worked for a man who never said thank you. He said that his boss only told him what he was doing wrong. Barry told us how he had become negative and bitter shortly after being hired. He remembers dreading going to work for "that son-of-a-bitch."

Five years later, Glenn replaced Barry's supervisor. Barry remembers that after the first shift, Glenn approached Barry and said he appreciated his help with a mechanical problem on some equipment that was unfamiliar to Glenn. Barry was surprised, but still skeptical. This must have been a fluke. Over the next few weeks, Glenn found many reasons to thank Barry, as well as the others on the crew.

Barry said he didn't even realize it, but his wife noticed that he didn't seem to mind going to work as much as he had in the past. She asked him why. He said he hadn't thought about it but that his supervisor, Glenn, just was a better guy to work for. Later he came home and said the biggest difference was that Glenn had the decency to say thank you.

Before we list the simple steps of acknowledging another, it is first important to understand the heart of the acknowledger. Gratitude must come from a sincere place. To understand and deliver a message of gratitude, the acknowledger must *feel* grateful. Therefore, a leader who wants to express gratitude, must *think* about what people are doing right. He must perceive the special gifts, the sacrifices, the dedication and attention that people bring to the workplace. He must constantly be looking for opportunities to express gratitude. Leaders sometimes have trouble getting the mindset right. Once the mindset is right, the gratitude follows easily.

Evelyn had risen through the ranks to become manager at a chemical company. She was driven to give the customer the best possible product and worked constantly to improve the operation. In her efforts to strive for the best, she was always evaluating the process, her employees, herself, and looking for ways to improve them all. The only way she knew to improve constantly was to look constantly for what was wrong. She criticized her own performance and that of everyone around her. She demanded better and higher levels of performance.

And it worked. Productivity was at the highest level ever. Unfortunately, morale was at its lowest. Interviews revealed over and over that people craved acknowledgment. Employees told us they were always told what they were doing wrong, but no one ever told them what they did right. No one ever said thank you.

When interviewing Evelyn, we discovered that she was grateful, but she simply didn't think to tell anyone. She said she was taught that she could always do better, that she should look constantly for ways to improve. Therefore, she always thought about what was wrong and not about what was right. Her focus on the negative meant she didn't feel grateful; she felt critical. So the message employees heard was criticism not gratitude.

Admittedly, this is not a simple shift for the leader. Years of conditioning had made her really good at criticizing. Therefore, changing her focus and recognizing her employees' sacrifices, then feeling grateful was not an easy task. But Evelyn saw the benefits of gratitude and committed herself to improvement. She decided that each day she would keep a "Gratitude List." She would write down examples of things, people, and accomplishments in the workplace that she was grateful for. In typical Evelyn fashion, she would criticize herself at two o'clock in the afternoon if her list was empty. Through criticism — which worked for her — Evelyn was able to change her behavior. After about a year of this practice, a surprising thing happened to Evelyn.

Evelyn told me that her thinking caused a dramatic life change. A year earlier, she had been on the verge of divorcing her husband, and her relationship with her teenage son was filled with confrontation and havoc. By looking for things to be grateful for at work, she automatically found herself looking for things to be grateful for at home. She admits that at first it was not only difficult, but that people were suspicious — even her husband and son. It took a long time and much persistence to break through this barrier. But eventually, her family responded to her transformation.

Most significantly, Evelyn said, "I am a different person, I think differently than I did a year ago. I am much happier and content with people in general. I force myself every day to take a good, hard look at all the good in people."

Everything isn't perfect at work yet. Some people still mistrust her motives, yet, a year later, most employees admit the atmosphere is much better. And productivity? It is at its highest point.

So how do we do it? It seems simple enough, yet over and over, I hear about good intentions that just don't deliver the gratitude message.

Betty has worked for a large manufacturer for more than 10 years. In those 10 years, Betty says, she had never heard a supervisor say thank you to her. She said that on occasion, management will tell the entire shift that they are doing a good job and to keep up the good work. But, Betty said that kind of acknowledgement almost feels like an insult. Betty explained that in the past ten years she had missed only five days of work. She said she is very conscientious about errors and scrap. She also makes it a point to be at her worksite early to get ready for the start of the shift and makes sure she cleans up her area at the end of her shift.

Some of her co-workers are less conscientious. Their error rate and scrap rate are very high. They miss a lot of work, and they do as little as possible to get by. She said that when management calls them all together and acknowledges everyone for doing a good job, she feels slighted. Hasn't anyone recognized that she is busting her tail, while others are on a free ride?

Remember, we're talking simple here. Don't over-complicate this genuine act of gratitude. All that it requires is:

- ❖ A sincere heart on the part of the leader

- ❖ A simple, specific statement of thanks to a specific person

- ❖ Explaining why you are grateful

- ❖ Delivered personally soon after the event

- ❖ Never mixed with a word of criticism or sarcasm

- ❖ Reinforced or linked back to values or expectations

- ❖ And delivered with "touch": eye contact; a warm, sincere voice; and a caring heart.

One contrast worth noting is the type of rote thank you we sometimes receive at the end of the check-out line or at the fast-food restaurant. "Thank you. Have a nice day," is delivered without eye contact to some nondescript person in a monotone voice aimed at fulfilling a job requirement and getting you out of the way so the next customer can be served. There is no gratitude attached to this message, nothing heartfelt.

> In contrast, I was at the grocery store with a rather large order. Every available clerk was busy, and the lines snaked halfway to the back of the store. Not out of the goodness of my heart, but rather due to my impatience, I bagged the groceries while the clerk was still checking my order. After everything was bagged, the clerk turned to me, looked me in the eye, and said very warmly, "Thanks, I really appreciate you bagging for me." Now, maybe I'm not very smart, and maybe I was being manipulated, but I'd bag for her anytime. I felt appreciated.

Through many workshops I've done titled "The Thank You Connection" or "The Gratitude Gate," I've found that my own reaction is typical. Most people have told me that when people or leaders say thank you, the most typical response was that people wanted to do more. People invariably said that it made them go out of their way to please others and to do a little extra. During my workshops, I have people list on flip charts how they feel when someone in the workplace sincerely says thank you, and in fact, the three categories of responses I get are:

1) It makes people want to do more (increases productivity).

2) It makes people feel good about themselves (increases self esteem).

3) It makes people feel good about the person delivering the thank you (improves relationships).

How many tools do we have that can increase productivity, enhance self-esteem, and improve relationships all in one sweep? How can we as leaders ignore the power of such a simple tool?

However, we must keep in mind that the true motive behind gratitude is simply to say "thank you." If this motive becomes corrupted, and gratitude is used simply for gain, then the leader is dishonest and his efforts will likely backfire.

Arnold told us about a leader he worked for who used gratitude when he wanted something and everyone knew it. He never said thank you unless he also asked for something in return. This obvious manipulation made employees more reluctant to please because they knew that they would probably be called on to do more.

Every trade requires its tool. Gratitude is no different. The tools of gratitude are quite simple. The most basic, yet most powerful, is your word. To say "thank you" sincerely and have it delivered with meaning, eye contact, and perhaps a handshake, is all that is needed for people to understand your gratitude. You can also add some variety to your thank-you message. Handwritten thank-you notes are a special way to say thank you. Keep a supply of interesting notes and stamps handy and make it a habit to send one a day, or one a week. I have learned that many people tend to save handwritten thank-you notes. In my office I have a small table where I collect thank-you notes that have been sent to me. I call it my gratitude table. It serves as a reminder that gratitude is a powerful way to repay someone for efforts. As I read the thank-you notes, it also makes me want to find other ways to help people.

One of my favorite ways to express gratitude is by handing people a $100 Grand candy bar along with a heartfelt thanks. It brings instant smiles to people's faces when I say, "Thank you, I really appreciate (whatever). Here's a $100 Grand just to let you know how grateful I am." I did this once to a policeman who was directing pedestrian and auto traffic on a busy corner. He stopped, looked at me, and asked, "Are you crazy, lady? No one ever thanks police officers." Then he grinned and tore open the wrapper.

Even the dreaded voice mail can serve as a powerful conveyor of gratitude. I had spent a hectic week training workers at a large financial institution, where I had imposed on the building crew numerous times to move furniture, retrieve supplies, move audio visuals, etc. When I got back to my office, I called the building manager, whom I had never met, and left a voice mail message thanking the building crew for being so cooperative and helpful. I explained in detail the kinds of things they had done that week and why I was so grateful. It took less than five minutes of my time. The building manager called his crew together in his office and played my voice mail message for them.

Later, he called me and thanked me for thanking them. He told me that people often take them for granted and that my call really lifted their spirits. I've gone back to that organization many times;

every time, the building crew has bent over backwards to help me in any way they can. Thank you, building crew. I appreciate your efforts.

A simple carnation can also say thank you and bring a smile to someone's face. A single flower expresses gratitude and beauty, which are closely connected. Gratitude brings out the inner beauty of both the giver and the receiver.

So the tools are simple. You can build self esteem, productivity, and relationships with a Hershey's Kiss, a $100 Grand candy bar, a carnation, a thank-you note, a phone call, or just your presence saying thank you for a job well done. Yes, it's the job we are paying people to do, and yes, that might be enough for some, but, what harm is there in spending a moment to honor a person with gratitude?

Through gratitude, leaders can begin to change the way a person perceives the workplace and job and ultimately, perhaps, elevate even the person's self-image — all this from the free gift of gratitude.

Gretchen revealed a touching story about the force that gratitude had in her life. She said she had always been burdened by feelings of inferiority. No matter what she did to overcome them, she just didn't feel confident in herself. Gretchen had a 20-year work history, and although she knew her supervisors liked her work, she never really felt good enough on the inside.

Her company launched a productivity and quality improvement process founded on the idea of teams. Facilitators drew people out using a variety of techniques and made sure the team members received the credit for any accomplishments.

Because of her low-key style, Gretchen would have preferred to sit quietly at the team meetings. However, the facilitators were adept at drawing out all team members' ideas and suggestions, including Gretchen's.

Time after time, the team implemented Gretchen's ideas, resulting in numerous quality and productivity improvements. In fact, over a two-year period, this team produced more hard-dollar results than all 17 other teams in the company combined. Each time, many people acknowledged the team's accomplishments. The team was gracious and always told others that special thanks belonged to Gretchen. Gretchen talks about the team experience as life changing. She said initially she felt disbelief. When accolades came her way via the team, she would quickly discount them. But the team wouldn't let her discount her contributions. Time after time, the team as well as management bombarded her with sincere gratitude for the accomplishments. Gretchen admits that she probably will never be 100% confident in her ability; however, she said that after hearing so many people acknowledge her contributions in the past two years, she is profoundly changed. She says she feels completely different on the inside.

Gratitude has the power to change the feelings and thoughts, not just the behaviors, of the people we lead. Changing feelings and thoughts are the seeds of inspiration. We begin to free people, to allow them to do their best, to create, to find their inner strength and beauty, and through gratitude, we encourage people to let it all shine through.

It also builds our organizations. Through gratitude, we give power to our expectations and our visions. We make it clear what we value and how individual contributors working together are the key to getting us closer to our goals and objectives.

Spirit Killers and Soul Suckers

GRATITUDE FOR GAIN

Beware. If the leader uses gratitude for gain or manipulation, people will see through her. We repeat: The sole purpose of gratitude is to honor the other person by acknowledging his effort, attitude, skill, or experience. Yes, we believe there are payoffs from expressing gratitude, but if the leader does this with the payoff in mind rather than the real purpose, the results will be corrupted. People will see it as merely a manipulation tool and will not respond in the same way.

USING DOLLARS TO MEASURE GRATITUDE

We also have more to gain if we separate gratitude from monetary rewards. Once we say thank you and here is $100 for your effort, then we begin to judge the effort. It could leave people thinking, "Well, if it was that good, why is it worth only $100, why not $200?" Gratitude isn't about money. It is about truly honoring people's efforts and sacrifices in the workplace with a heartfelt thank you. Fair rewards and compensation surely have a place in an organization, but I would prefer that we think of them separately so as not to contaminate the purity of gratitude. It should be a message from one heart to another. Besides, so many monetary reward programs are formal, lag the effort, and require paperwork and approvals. All of that is contrary to the way gratitude must be delivered.

BLIND GRATITUDE

In addition to pairing gratitude and monetary reward, another mistake can kill the good intentions of gratitude. Sometimes leaders don't see clearly. Perhaps the leader sees that Paolo has done a great job on a project and tells him so. Unfortunately, he hasn't seen Phillip's efforts to make the project a success. In his efforts to recognize Paolo, the leader could have made Phillip feel hurt or unappreciated.

REDUNDANT GRATITUDE

Not again please. This leader thanks everyone for everything every minute of the day. The beauty of the word 'thank you' is distorted due to overuse. Acknowledgment must be targeted in order for the receiver to gain.

INSINCERE GRATITUDE

Don't say thank you if you don't mean it. Employees will know instantly if you are insincere. It's best not to say anything. It will only ruin your credibility if you say things you don't mean.

Dear Supervisor,

You made my day yesterday. To you, it was probably a non-event, but I actually went home and told my husband and daughters about what a great day I had.

When you came over and said thank you to me for helping Mr. Cosumics, you really made me feel good. You said you appreciated what I did. You said that you knew Mr. Cosumics was a difficult customer, but also an important customer. You said I did a great job.

Thank you so much for recognizing that I really do try. I come in and I really want to please you. I want to make our customers happy. Thanks for noticing.

Sincerely,

Betty

My Dear Boss,

I've worked for you for a long time now, yet I don't really understand you. You know that I always come through, yet somehow, I never get the impression that it matters to you.

Remember last quarter when we had a major backlog? Who stayed until midnight for six days in a row to make sure the shipment was intact? What about last week when the accounts didn't balance? I was right there piecing together the paperwork and tracking the errors. I feel as though I show you every day that I care about this place. Yet, not once have you ever said thank you. Instead, you complained yesterday when I said that I couldn't stay overtime because my son had a doctor's appointment. Another issue that confuses me is why you always ask me to do things and don't ask some of the others. It's as if I am being punished because I do a good job.

I'm not going to stop doing a good job because you don't say thank you. That's not in my nature. But, why can't you tell me sometimes that you are grateful? It would mean a lot.

For every action, these is an equal and opposite reaction.

Sir Issac Newton

4. CONTRIBUTIONS

Equal and Fair Contributions

Imagine it's Saturday, your day off. You've worked hard all week. As you look around the house, you realize you have heaps of laundry to do and the grass to cut. You haven't a morsel of food in the house to eat, and the dog needs to go to the vet. This list doesn't include the mold growing in the shower nor the dust accumulating on the floors. Finally, your brother has just called and asked if you could help him with his resume. You're overwhelmed, but as usual, you dig in.

In the same scenario, what if your spouse or significant other decides, as usual, to take the day off. She decides it's a great day for a bike ride in the mountains, so she loads the car and waves good-bye. Feeling any pangs of resentment?

Suppose you've grown up in a household where every Saturday morning, the whole family parks themselves in front of the TV and laughs together over the weekly selection of cartoons. You believe that this weekly laughter ritual strengthens the soul and makes the rest of life bearable. Afterwards, you're eager to spend the afternoon digging into chores. However, your spouse believes that Saturday *mornings* were created for chores. Get up early and get them done before noon, and then life is worth living. Do you think this might cause some problems?

Or maybe it's your teen-age daughter who comes home from school and makes herself a peanut butter and jelly sandwich. You come home from work a couple of hours later, and as usual, discover the peanut butter and jelly knife stuck to the counter, the milk carton left out, and bread crumbs marking the trail to her room where she drowns out the sound of your objections with her latest CD.

Or maybe your boss comes in and asks you to stay late to finish her financial report because she has guests coming over for dinner and she would like to get home early.

What if you notice three of your employees casually relaxing by the vending machines when you just came back from the production meeting and had to explain why your numbers are behind this week?

Whether in our personal relationships or our business relationships, our natural tendency as humans is to look for equity and fairness. We want to believe that all parties contribute equally to the whole. If anyone perceives otherwise, then the seeds of resentment and, ultimately, mistrust are born.

Sometimes you hear the following comments reflecting people's thoughts about workplace contributions. If you hear these comments often, they may indicate warning signs for management. They don't necessarily mean that inequities exist; they might indicate there is a perception of inequity. Do these sound familiar?

EMPLOYEES:

❖ All they do is sit in meetings. They don't even know what we do.

❖ When we have a problem, my supervisor walks away. He doesn't care. He just tells me to solve it. What the hell do I have a supervisor for?

❖ Management just takes care of themselves; they don't care about us.

❖ They expect us to do all the work while they go golfing.

❖ All they ever do is push for more and more from us. Yet, they never lift a finger; they just point them.

MANAGEMENT:

❖ If we're not out there watching over things, nothing gets done.

❖ Why do I have to solve all of their problems?

❖ We're paying them to think. Why don't they start doing it?

❖ We're not paying people to sit around. We're paying them to work. We're tired of their nonchalant attitudes.

❖ There is no sense of urgency with our employees. All of the burden is on us.

The astute leader brings harmony and understanding so everyone in the workplace believes everyone is contributing equally. "Equal" doesn't mean the same. If people believe that each person contributes a fair amount of work, that the work the other does has value and that it contributes to the health of the business, then we have equity. However, we all know this is more easily said than done.

The Leaders' Actions and Reactions

ON A SIMPLE LEVEL,
LET'S CONSIDER THIS INCIDENT:

At an industrial plant along the river, a new employee was moving a large drum of liquid soap. It rolled off the forklift and was punctured by the prong of the lift, spilling highly concentrated liquid soap all over the asphalt pavement. Located near the spill was a rainwater run-off drain. The supervisor came by and told the employee to clean up the spill quickly and be sure that as much of the soap as possible was cleared away. As the supervisor scurried away on his cart, the new employee grabbed the nearby water hose and hosed the asphalt clean. Not a trace of the soap remained. About an hour later, the plant received a call from the Environmental Protection Agency. As it turned out, the run-off drain led directly to the river. Large foamy clouds of soap suds were cruising down the river in direct violation of the EPA, resulting in hefty fines for the company.

A review of this incident produces many questions.

Should the supervisor have given a more detailed explanation?

Should the employee have asked for clarification?

Should the supervisor have asked a more experience person to do the job?

Should the supervisor have provided a more experienced person to train the employee?

There are many obvious learning points from this simple story. It is easy to deduce what should have been done, and in doing so, we can learn important messages about communications and delegation.

However, equally important, if not more so, are the reactions to efforts that go awry. These reactions provide deep insight for leaders. They also provide a study of the messages that we send each day to employees.

Should management have disciplined or even fired the new employee?

Should management have disciplined or even fired the supervisor?

Should management have thanked the new employee for working so diligently to clear the spill?

Should management have commended the new employee for acting and thinking independently?

Should management have commended the supervisor for fostering an environment that allows people to think independently?

Each of these reactions sends different underlying messages that affect the culture and set expectations for the next situation. Yet, if this one incident can send so many messages, imagine, daily, weekly, how many messages we send. The leader's behavior, both in setting expectations up front and in reacting to situations in the workplace, tells followers over and over what is important. Employees use these messages to draw conclusions. They draw conclusions about fairness and equity, about management's honesty, about management's contributions and their own contributions, and about the type of organization that greets them each day as they walk through the gate.

Take a Stand

> *You've got to be brave and you've got to be bold.*
> *Brave enough to take your chance*
> *on your own discrimination —*
> *what's right and what's wrong*
> *what's good and what's bad.*

Robert Frost

If you stop and think about it, it's amazing that any of us can live and work together. There is so much opportunity for confusion, ambiguity, and downright resentment regarding contributions and expectations.

Confusion and ambiguity regarding acceptable behavior disappear when the leader takes a stand.

In one quick sweep, I witnessed a firm, clear act of setting expectations with a rowdy group of factory workers. John, a newly appointed plant manager, proceeded to meet with groups of workers to listen to concerns and complaints. In a business-as-usual manner, the workers attacked the new plant manager, using foul language, making degrading remarks about members of management, and raising their voices in a mob-like scene.

John listened long enough to get the flavor of the discussion and then suddenly put a halt to the ruckus. He said, "Look, this kind of personal attack, foul language, and disrespect divides us as a plant. I do not intend to treat you in a disrespectful way and I do not want this kind of treatment for me or members of management. I am here to help us together build a better future at this plant, and this kind of behavior does not contribute to that goal. I will talk with you about any issue, any time, but not in this manner. I expect us to treat each other in a civil way."

Then, he promptly ended the meeting. All of a sudden, this leader put a stop to behavior that had gone on for quite some time at this plant. As time passed, the leader also showed that he meant what he said. In a civil tone, he would address any issue with truth and sincerity the factory workers presented.

Here the leader speaks about acceptable behavior. His actions support his belief. If, however, he demands respectable behavior but disrespects his employees, he not only destroys his credibility and trust, he unites employees in their cynicism.

Let's take a look at how good intentions can easily fall apart.

Connie had made it clear to her management team that for this organization to survive, it needed to reestablish bonds with the union. The best way to do that would be by treating employees with respect. Employees' most frequent complaint when Connie took over as president was that management did not treat them with respect. The workers provided her with numerous examples to support their claim. Management personnel routinely shouted at them in front of customers, called them names such as "dumb ass" in front of co-workers, and insulted their abilities in section meetings. Connie promised the union that she would address this matter.

Armed with loads of examples from her "Let's Talk" sessions with employees, Connie called a special management meeting. She started the meeting by listing comments on the flip chart. The flip chart read:

1.) "You dumb ass, it's the belt that's slipping!"

2.) "Are you going to sit on your ass or go and get material to work on?"

3.) "If I were as mechanically inclined as you, I think I would have chosen to become a hairdresser."

4.) "I'd give you a blueprint, but I know you couldn't read it."

5.) "Get George to help you. At least he knows a wrench from a winch."

6.) "Are you waiting for an invitation to wait on this customer?"

Connie grabbed a giant-sized red marker and drew a circle with a slash through it. She asked, "Do you understand? It is not acceptable to treat people like this. It shows lack of respect. WE MUST STOP DOING THIS NOW."

Throughout the year, she reminded her management team of the significance of respecting employees. She also set an excellent example with her team, treating them with respect and caring.

Many of the management group bought in and worked to ensure they were upholding these values. However, the person in charge of nearly two-thirds of the hourly workforce continued to operate as usual. Unfortunately, this person had been the primary offender in the first place. A year later, when Connie conducted her annual employee "Let's Talk" sessions, employees were downright hostile. Sadly, Connie was out of touch with employees during the year and she believed that she had addressed the situation by discussing her expectations with the management group. This kind of blind trust on the part of the leader regarding the management team was misplaced.

So clear, consistent expectations from the leader are important. However, it is also vitally important that other members of the leader's management team uphold the same values. Connie made the mistake of not monitoring. She took a stand, then sat down. If you're going to be the leader, you need to keep standing.

The Value of Values

Values are the toughest and the most important issue for leaders to address. Values can have a powerful impact on what workers do every day. Although clear expectations are important at all levels and will help people do the right things, values, both our personal values and the group values, are the most significant influence in determining our actions.

Once values expectations are firmly established within the workplace, employees will often react to behavior that threatens a value. I watched a heartwarming example of how peers worked to maintain a level of respect and politeness in their workplace in the following situation.

Every week, workers jammed the conference room to meet with section management. The meetings gave everyone a chance to step back and look at how things were going. The usual meeting produced a list of issues on the flip charts that needed attention, discussion regarding the course of action, and an action for someone.

Harry, the section supervisor, put up the list from the previous meeting. It included:

1) The supply house didn't have the right kind of flippers for machine two / Sue would check with the purchasing manager.

2) The load was uneven on Wednesday / Jim and Ted would look into the problem and see if it could have been prevented and report at the next meeting.

3) The safety guard on pocket three was broken /
Harry would call maintenance and put in a work order.

As Harry began to review the progress, I could see
Shawn's agitation. His neck veins bulged, he stood up and
attacked Harry. "I'm sick of this. These meetings are a
waste of time. Management is a bunch of assholes. I'm
sick of sitting in these meetings, telling you what the problems are, and then you ignoring the most important thing
on the list. And this isn't the first time. Don't waste my
time anymore." Shawn stormed out of the room.

Stunned by the outburst, some co-workers
exchanged glances, others put their eyes to the ground,
Harry looked at the flip chart and then looked around the
room. A cloud hung in the air. No one wanted to be the
first to speak.

Finally, Harry gently and humbly said he thought
Shawn was entitled to his opinion. For the next half hour,
the remaining employees talked about the fact that people
are indeed entitled to their opinions, but that they
expected their co-workers or management or anyone else
who entered their workplace to state their opinions in a
respectful way. Management learned later that several
people had approached Shawn and told him that he owed
his co-workers and management an apology. This same
group developed a code of conduct for future meetings
that reflected their desire to keep respect in their
workplace.

Later in the day, Harry asked Shawn about the incident. Shawn said that since the safety guard was still broken on pocket three, he thought Harry hadn't followed through. Shawn said that management shouldn't promise to do something and not follow through, especially on safety issues. In fact, Harry had put the maintenance order in. He wasn't aware that the guard had not been fixed. Shawn apologized for his outburst. He said he had lost his temper and hoped Harry could forgive him.

Unfortunately, on the contrary, I have watched this same type of peer reaction to values result in a negative environment and in value norms that defied good business practice. In fact, in my experience, the following type of support for values from peers is more typical.

John was eager to start at the brewery and wanted to make a good impression. He considered himself fortunate to be working for such a good company. His thought his pay and benefits were good and wanted to give the company a good day's work for the money.

After a couple of weeks on the job, John felt like a master. The once-intimidating equipment purred in his hands. As he became more familiar with the job and the environment, he noticed that employees often had to reload the lids on a certain size bottling machine because the cap holders got stuck. John designed a way to fix the cap holders so this wouldn't happen again. Also, after a while, John noticed that he could load and bottle as fast as anyone there. In fact, each day, he noticed that his production figures made him either the top producer or very close to the top.

One day in the lunchroom as John washed down a ham and cheese sandwich, a couple of co-workers sat down and joined him. They clearly and quietly explained the "rules" to him. They did it because they cared about him and they didn't want him to get in any trouble with anyone. Besides, they explained, the rules helped everyone. By working at a slower pace, no one would be laid off. Also, cap holder designs were for engineering to think about. They don't pay us to think about designs. The co-workers stayed long enough to make sure that John understood. They carefully communicated the shared values that were in place so that John would be sure to "fit in."

So how does the leader ensure that the "right" values are in place? By "right," I mean values that work toward the business goals. It takes hard work and a conscious effort by the leaders to change and manage group values. This cannot be left to chance.

Leaders must ask critical questions such as: "What values are important?" and "Changed to what?"

The answer to these important questions transforms an organization. Instead of the law of the jungle, an effective, moral code guides everyone's behavior.

To answer these questions, leaders must carefully analyze the messages — to complete the circle — they send each day. Consider this example:

> At a manufacturing plant that produces molded plastic containers, material is cycled through many different pieces of equipment in order to produce the final product. Four minutes in machine A, three minutes in machine B, nine minutes in machine C. Barring any machine difficulties or material problems, the whole process is quite predictable. Management knew it could expect an experienced operator to produce a certain number of pieces per hour. Yet, let's assume that a few operators decided not to trouble themselves to make the numbers. What do you suppose could happen if management turns its back to these few operators and ignores the problem?

In our work environments, the leader's actions value or devalue contributions. These actions send strong messages to employees. In the scenario above, the following interpretations could result:

❖ If management doesn't care, why should I?

❖ Management isn't doing its job. It ignores poor performance.

❖ I'm not going to bust my butt if my co-workers aren't expected to.

❖ They let some people get away with slacking off. That's not fair.

These perceptions seed distrust. The perceptions grow from the leader's actions and inaction. If, however, the leader decides up front that equity and fairness are important, and measures all of his decisions against this value, then it's likely that his actions would engender fairness. But first, he must decide what values he values in the workplace. Then, these values serve as the moral foundation for doing business.

But What if People Aren't Contributing?

It all seems so simple. Just decide on the shared workplace values that will make your organization a better and more successful place, clearly and consistently communicate the expectations in a respectful way, and we all live happily ever after in the Land of Oz. Who said life was difficult?

Unfortunately, it doesn't work that way. Along the path, you as the leader will encounter — or have already — many challenging situations. Some of the situations will be of your own making. You'll forget to follow some of the basics, or other aspects of humanness will surface that may take you off course. You may also encounter conflicts that, when resolved, will give you tremendous gifts and enhance your organization — *if* you pay attention to their lessons. It is also possible that you will not be able to resolve some conflicts in a win-win manner.

Darryl worked in a technical job for a non-technical manager. He was working on cutting-edge technology. Technical problems delayed projects and put pressure on the manager. From the manager's point of view, Darryl wouldn't, because he was so introverted, try to find solutions by consulting with others who were doing similar work. The manager did this himself to try to help solve problems on several projects, but this seemed really senseless for two reasons:

1) Darryl was ultimately the one who had to speak to the resource because the problem was highly technical.

2) The manager had other things to do with his time instead of doing Darryl's job.

The manager opened the coaching session with touch. He could see that Darryl was defeated over the problems, and he knew that Darryl had tried all of the solutions he could think of, but to no avail.

He opened with, "Darryl, I can see that you are really worried about this problem."

Darryl acknowledged as much and said that he was even waking up in the middle of the night trying to come up with a solution. The manager persisted to discuss the impact that the problem was having on Darryl and how difficult it must be for him. He did not talk about missed deadlines and unhappy customers. Darryl knew about that already.

The manager then persisted to place importance on Darryl and the project. He acknowledged that what he was doing was difficult and that there weren't many people doing this type of work. It was no wonder that Darryl had encountered so many problems.

The manager continued. "You know Darryl, I wish I could actually give you the answer, but I can't, I just don't know enough about what you are doing. The best I can do is offer resources for you to try."

Darryl was touched, he felt strengthened and supported by his manager. Little by little, he reached out and developed a network of peers to help solve problems. Each time he did, he was reinforced by his manager and strengthened even more.

A traditional coaching session with Darryl would have looked different. The manager would have restated the need to reach the deadline and solve the problem. He may have asked for Darryl's opinion on how to do this, then proceeded to offer the resources that might help. Depending on how much pressure he felt, Darryl may have worked a few more days on his own, further delaying the project if no solution was forthcoming, or he may have contacted the resource because he thought he had no other choice. But surely, this would have been a temporary fix. The next problem would more than likely have resulted in the same type of behavior on Darryl's part.

The important thing to keep in mind when coaching is to do it with the ultimate aim of touching the inside of the person in order to make a lasting impact on the way the person thinks. Coaching with touch isn't about changing behavior. Changing behavior is simply a by-product of this type of coaching. Coaching with touch is about building people's beliefs, values, and self-esteem as they relate to work. Some people have a knack for doing this. These people tend to believe in reaching inside others and giving them strength and insight. Coaching with touch can change the person because it reaches inside the heart and soul and says: "This can be better, and I will support you. All you need to do is try."

Coaching with touch requires a genuine heart. However, a genuine heart doesn't mean that the leader ignores the truth. If the reality is poor performance or intolerable conduct, the leader with the genuine heart must face these unpleasant truths. The genuine heart helps the leader to address these issues with honesty and caring. The purpose is to help the employee meet the demands of the job, not to fire him. In this spirit, the leader will offer help and assistance where possible. It doesn't mean that the leader helps by taking on this person's responsibilities himself or by shifting the responsibilities to another person. It means he honestly confronts the issues and works with the individual to enable success.

In the short term, fear and intimidation work quite well to change behavior. But to change the inside – the thinking process and belief system that drives the individual – will require the leader to enter with the exact opposite approach. The leader must become someone whom the employee honors if he is to influence the inside. Honor can't be achieved through fear and intimidation.

In a fascinating interview with a work crew in a manufacturing plant, I learned the game of "bully." The workers talked about several front-line supervisors they had had over the years, and I asked them whether or not their performance varied from supervisor to supervisor. They told me that the inside joke was to see how long it would take "to get the bully out." They explained that they would drag their feet and their production numbers to see how long it would take to get the supervisor to scream and yell, or otherwise "bully" them to work. Then they would belly laugh and compare notes on the boiling point of this collection of supervisors.

One creative individual even constructed a chart, similar to the production charts, that kept track of the bully points. It was part of their culture and heritage in this department. Then one day, a supervisor from another department was transferred in. This supervisor had a good reputation and knew about the "bully" game. He worked every day to touch the crew. He worked individually with each member to get to know him. He constantly asked for their input on how production could improve. He listened to their concerns and he followed up on their suggestions. He rewarded many of their suggestions and always gave attention and praise to them.

Interestingly, the crew said that a few of them wanted to play the "bully" game with him, and pressured others to drag their feet, but it didn't work. Too many people felt a personal bond with and responsibility to this leader, and they didn't think it would be right to "pull his chain." This was a fascinating tribute to the power of touch, and the whole crew felt it. They placed honor at the feet of their leader. They chose to change their behavior from the inside out.

When approaching conflicts related to values, the leader must be especially sensitive. It is easy to come across preachy or high brow in this type of matter. Setting strong examples, trying to understand the other person's perspective, and tolerating occasional bouts of being human, will help the leader to understand, coach, and build cultures that reflect the shared values.

In an organization known for showing customers respect, an employee was overheard being rude to a customer on the telephone. This company had established customer orientation and service as a shared value. The employees understood that:

❖ The customer was their livelihood.

❖ Their reputation for customer service was the reason that they were No. 1 in their industry.

❖ Their customers had many other choices in the marketplace.

❖ Management supported employees trying to help customers.

So how would managament coach this employee who was rude to the customer?

Mary, the supervisor, spoke with Jennifer about the incident. She opened the conversation by saying she understood that sometimes working in customer service can be stressful and said that it is especially difficult because sometimes customers can make us angry. She told Jennifer that she had overheard her lose her temper with a customer. She listened as Jennifer described the conflict and why the customer had made her angry. Mary said she understood why Jennifer may have felt angry. Together they talked about why that can hurt business. She asked Jennifer what kind of service makes her feel most valued as a customer. Mary was careful not to preach, but instead treated Jennifer with respect. Mary constantly reinforced the value of customer service in her talk with Jennifer. She asked if there was anything she could do to help Jennifer ward off those angry feelings with the customer. Jennifer laughed and said that maybe they could screen calls and only send her the pleasant ones. They talked about some of the techniques that were discussed in the "Dealing With Angry Customers" seminar that had been held a few months earlier. Jennifer apologized for the incident and said that she would keep her temper under control.

Obviously, I was speaking here of a situation in which the employee(s) has the skills necessary, but for whatever reason, is not performing appropriately. In the case of a person who does not have the skill to perform the job, the leader with the caring heart will go out of her way to make sure the employee is given all the training and education she needs to perform. She does this without blame or shame and encourages the individual to learn.

Most people respond to this kind of coaching. Whether the problem is due to a "can't do" or a "won't do," coaching with touch can make an impression. Coaching with touch demands that the leader include basic tenants, such as listening, respect, caring, and two-way communication. This may be just the kind of touch the "won't do's" were waiting for. Also, people who "can't do" the job or meet the expectation, may just need this additional touch to have the confidence and self-esteem to learn whatever is keeping them from success. Unfortunately, sometimes, despite the most genuine efforts, people do not respond.

A brave decision on the part of one company's management clearly communicated and upheld the workplace values.

When George had taken over about a year earlier, his crew were at each other's throats. They were acting petty and competitive. Some members didn't even speak to each other. George clearly established the workplace values he expected. These included things like teamwork, open communications, and respect. Together, the work group and George defined the behaviors that reflected these values. After a long year of coaching with touch, and recoaching with touch, restating the expectations, defining and redefining acceptable behaviors that reflected the defined values, these people were humming. They were a TEAM, except for Nicole.

George had spent numerous hours with Nicole. He had tried every way he could think of to help her to become part of the team. Unfortunately, she just didn't get it. Over and over, her behaviors were downright destructive. She tried to pull people apart, she constantly talked about others, she tried to inflame others by spreading rumors. It was a constant "he said this about you, why don't you and he fight" type of environment that this woman tried to create. No amount of coaching was making an impact.

As George tried with a genuine heart to pull her into the team, finally, after a great deal of frustration, he began documenting his discussions with Nicole. Eventually, he gave her a verbal warning. Finally, George fired Nicole for conduct that was not conducive to the workplace team. The corporate attorneys were nervous. This person had excellent job stats. Her production was above average. But the case was well documented and George's boss understood and supported the dismissal. The company took a stand on workplace values.

After Nicole was terminated, the team sent George a note. The note was signed by every team member. The note read: "George, we know you tried with Nicole. It's not your fault. She had the same choice we all had. You were more than fair with her."

Yes, she brought a wrongful discharge suit. To avoid litigation, the company settled out of court. In this instance, it was worth the fee to make the values statement.

The leader's job is particularly difficult when things go wrong and expectations aren't met. However, this is also the time when the organization most needs a leader. His actions at this point can make the difference that sends lasting messages to the workforce. The way the leader addresses these situations will communicate the soul that people come to associate with the company. If these situations are addressed with a genuine heart, filled with caring and compassion and touch, balanced firmly and fairly with the business needs in mind, then, and only then, will the leader be doing his job.

Spirit Killers and Soul Suckers

EXPECTATIONS THAT APPLY ONLY TO SOME

Perhaps as adults we should be above such things as comparing our circumstances to those of our peers, but we aren't. Most people despair if they see themselves meeting expectations that others are not required to. Besides the ill feelings that are created among co-workers, an atmosphere of inequity leads to mistrust. That's not to say there aren't exceptions to the rules, but those exceptions should be clear and reasonable.

WIMPY LEADERS

Some leaders are just wimps. They are afraid to take a stand and say "this is right in our workplace" or "this is wrong in our workplace." The world of leaders has no room for wimps. Take a stand. Even if you're wrong, at least people won't be confused. And if you are wrong, and sincerely admit it, many people will understand and respect you for admitting your error.

In the following example, one leader did a great deal to clarify expectations and gain respect by admitting he made a mistake and then immediately correcting it.

Richard was one of three staff managers at a envelope manufacturer of about 400 people. The staff managers had worked hard over the past two years to gain more involvement and interaction with the middle-level management team. The staff managers included middle managers in decisions. Consensus had become a way of life for the team. One day, the three staff managers made an important decision that affected the entire plant. There had been no discussion or consultation with the middle managers.

Over lunch one day, Jeff confronted his boss, Richard, about the decision and the fact that no middle managers had been consulted. He told Richard he wasn't objecting to the decision, but to the exclusion of the middle managers from the process. Jeff pointed out the hypocrisy. Richard put his fork down, stopped eating, and listened to Jeff. After Jeff finished, Richard picked up his fork and said, "Jeff, I hate to admit this, but you are absolutely right." He didn't say another word about the situation to Jeff. He simply resumed eating his lunch.

Immediately after lunch, Richard called the two other staff managers together and told them about his luncheon conversation. Richard suggested they immediately meet with the middle managers and discuss the issue and, if need be, change the decision based on the consensus of the group. The other two staff managers balked. But Richard, who is not usually a forceful person, insisted. He talked about how they had struggled to include the team in decisions, and how leaving the middle managers out had violated the trust they had placed in the group. Richard reminded them of the shared values they had adopted and how as keepers of the values, they were reneging on the expectations they had said were important. The other two managers finally agreed that it was the right thing to do.

They called the team together and Richard opened with the following statement, "I would like to thank Jeff for helping me understand that we have made a serious mistake. Last week, we made a decision without even consulting any of you. That was against the values that we are trying to instill. The purpose of today's meeting is to apologize for that error and to revisit the decision. We would like to come to a consensus regarding this decision."

The team was delighted. It took courage to admit the mistake, but the managers strengthened the bonds of trust that day.

NO FOLLOW THROUGH

Some leaders do an excellent job to ensure that all employees understand the contribution levels expected, but never follow through to reinforce the expectations. Not following through is essentially the same as not having any expectations. This simply leaves to chance the expectations that will take root in the workplace.

Dear Boss,

You know that it isn't fair, yet you do it every single day. You know I won't say no, like Joe and Alice and Harry, so you keep piling things on my desk that they have refused to do.

It's not fair! I am really tired of it. I feel like you are using me. I also heard that Harry gets twenty-five cents an hour more than me. How can you justify that? Every time you ask him to do something he says he's busy with the proof. So what do you do? You come over and put it on my desk.

One of these days, I'm going to quit. I can't quit now because I have to finish school. But when I'm done, I'm out of here.

Aline

Dear Manager,

Can you explain to me just why it has to be in your time and in your way? I am a very hard worker. My numbers prove it. Last month, my production figures were #1. That was the third straight month in a row in case you haven't noticed.

Yet, I just get the sense that you don't trust me. You ride me and I just hate that. If you would just leave me alone, I'll produce even more. Do you realize that every day at 9:15 A.M. you tell me I am behind? There is a reason for that, but I doubt you would want to hear it. If I take a few minutes in the morning, I can set up my station and that keeps me productive all day.

What I can't understand is why don't you ask Jeremy about his numbers? He's been on the bottom of the production heap for over four months. Why don't you go and find out how you can help him instead of wasting your time every day telling me that I am behind? I just don't get it.

Kevin

The Second Key

SHOW THE DREAM,
TALK THE DREAM,
LIVE THE DREAM

INTRODUCTION

CHART A COURSE, SET A DIRECTION, and commit your energy to it. Too often, employees told us tales of leaders who were afraid to commit to a path or didn't have a clue which path to take. If they did know which direction they were going, they kept it to themselves.

MOST WORKERS WANT THREE THINGS:

1. Workers want to know the big picture.

- ❖ 74% of workers didn't think they understood the company's mission or vision

- ❖ 84% of workers thought their performance could be improved if management gave them more information

As the leader shares her vision, the big picture becomes clearer to employees. It's up-front and spoken, not hidden and therefore, subject to suspicion. It also serves as a guidepost for actions. The vision becomes a compass that points the direction.

Sharing the big picture also honors the workers' status. It states, "You are important. You are an adult and we want to treat you as such."

On the simplest level, workers voiced frustration when they were trained how to perform a small function or piece of the process without being told how the small piece fits into the whole. It rendered them impotent for problem solving or troubleshooting effectively because they didn't understand the big picture.

2. Workers want some level of inclusion.

* 85% of workers said they would be willing to give ideas or opinions about how to improve things if they were asked by management

* 58% of workers thought that their opinions and suggestions fall on deaf management ears

Good leaders paint mental pictures of the future. They leave room however, for people to bring their own artist brushes and fill in the details on the canvas.

By including others, it increases honor. It says you value your workers. The true power here comes from treating people as adults. By improving this sense of importance, the overall trust improves.

Equal power comes from the fact that your entire workforce can now work toward the vision. Vision kills the scattered misconceptions that often abound regarding the direction. It enables people to unleash their creativity toward a singular direction.

3. Workers want to believe that the leader is equally (or more so) committed.

❖ Workers thought 31% of their leaders just go through the motions each day

❖ 39% of workers thought their immediate supervisors did not set a good example of commitment and passion for the job

Commitment and passion say, "Do as I do." It sets the example and serves as a model for workers. The leader's commitment must be genuine and visible. If people doubt the leader's interest, this just gives way for others to lack commitment.

Our interviewees weren't looking for passion in rousing speeches. Instead, they were searching for leaders who believe in what they are doing, rather than cardboard cutouts who go through the motions each day.

Setting the vision, including and inviting others to live the vision, and being passionate about the journey is the stuff that leadership is made of.

If you can't see it, it isn't.

If you can see it, it is.

---

5. VISION

Seeing Clearly — Developing Vision

What enables some people to look at a hunk of marble and see a statue, while others just see the marble? To see possibilities, to dream, and to imagine – that's the stuff visions are made of. Visions are not about goals. They are much larger than goals. They are mental pictures of the future. These pictures clearly place the organization in a new reality. The person with vision sees the reality *before* it exists. The fact is – if you can't see it, it isn't. If you can see it, it has the possibility to become.

Mission answers the question: "What are you called to do?" It considers what you are all about as an organization. What is your purpose? What is your place with your customers? What do you want to become? What do you value as an organization? What is your place in society? However, vision gives the mission a picture in its ideal. Employees can "see" the future of the organization because of the words and pictures that the leader uses to make it come alive.

To understand vision, let's imagine it on a personal level. One night, as you and your spouse or significant other linger with a cup of coffee after dinner, your spouse says she would like to become a major political influence in the United States or perhaps even the world. You think to yourself, "*That's great! Go vote!*" Does this statement have much impact for you? Can you see a "major political influence?"

What if, instead, your spouse or significant other said that she would like to become president of the United States in the year 2012? Is the vision clearer?

What if this spouse or significant other added to the vision by explaining that a major plank in her platform would be education reform. What if she went on to describe a system that would extend the role of colleges and universities? All students beginning in kindergarten and continuing through grade 12 would attend a university instead of the public school system as we know it? What if she included specific ideas of how she would bring about this vision? Would this vision be clearer? Would this statement have more impact for you? Vision must be clear enough so that people can imagine their place in it. Can you imagine your place in your spouse's vision of becoming a "major political influence?" What activities can you see yourself engaged in? Can you more clearly imagine your place as first husband, married to a U.S. president whose major political initiative is education reform? What activities can you see now?

A vivid vision allows room for people to bring their own artist's brushes and fill in the details on the canvas. The follower may need the leader's help to imagine a flower on the canvas, yet, it's the follower who will paint the flower, perhaps even an entire flower bed. Inspired by the leader's vision, yet not limited only to the leader's view, the results may well surpass the vision. This type of involvement with the vision allows others to become inspired and connected to the vision.

Kristine was the director of Admissions at a major hospital. She constantly heard from patients who described a cumbersome admissions process. Patients complained about waiting for long periods of time in uncomfortable chairs. Patients said they felt like they were no more than a number and that the paperwork took priority over their health.

Kristine called her staff together and explained her vision for a new way of processing admissions. Kristine's vision started with the patients. Kristine asked the staff to see the patients as important guests who were quite ill and who were visiting their home. She asked that they think of these guests as important people whom they loved. Her vision included pampering these guests, not badgering them for information. She asked them to imagine how they would want these special guests to be greeted, initially cared for, and otherwise "processed" into the hospital.

Kristine's vision set the framework: welcoming, pampering, and loving guests. From here, the staff began to see themselves in the vision. Simple acts such as assigning greeters to greet the guest at the door and dispensing stuffed animals to sick children changed the patient's view and the staff's view regarding the admission. They arranged first for the guest's comforts and immediate needs and then collected the data they needed. Complex changes regarding pre-admissions procedures and emergency admissions also followed.

Kristine's initial vision revolutionized the way admissions were processed. However, it was the staff who put the details and their signature to the vision.

Everyone's activities should connect to make the vision a reality. Your role as a leader is to invite people to think in terms of the vision. If you can coach them to think in the direction of the vision, they will become a part of its creation.

The worst sin of a leader may be having no vision at all. After all, bringing vision to the organization is a primary responsibility of leadership. Organizations without vision create confusion, discontent, and often bring rise to poor performance.

Imagine that you work for Medical Supply Company A. Your role is to fill orders. The procedure says that you fill orders by date and time stamp on a first-in, first-out basis. Orders are mailed or faxed. That's easy enough. When the phone rings and a customer needs a supply immediately, what do you do? You're not even sure you should answer the phone. Your job is to fill orders.

On the other hand, let's say that you work for Medical Supply Company B. Your role is to fill orders. The procedures are identical to Medical Supply Company A — first-in, first-out basis on mail or fax orders. However, at Medical Supply Company B, your boss, your boss's boss, and her boss, have all told you time and again that you are in the business of saving lives, not filling orders. Medical Supply Company B tells you that the priority is to save lives by ensuring that all customers have the needed supplies for their health and well-being. These customers, who could be your mother or grandmother, are sick or dying and in need of critical medical supplies. When a customer calls and needs a supply immediately, what do you do?

Visions give followers parameters. Visions don't give specific procedures. Instead, they give people a framework in which to think or view situations. Visions help empower people. They help eliminate confusion. Organizations that tend to have a procedure for everything may better spend their time deciding and communicating their vision. Don't misinterpret; procedures serve an important role. However, don't try to substitute a procedure for a vision.

One former Army captain working in industry vented his frustration regarding lack of vision. Plagued by takeovers and no fewer than six reorganizations in the past four years, his business unit was in shambles. He said as a foot soldier, he was looking to the front of the battalion for the leader. He was looking for the flag. He saw it when he looked to the East. So the next day, he looked to the East because that's where he had seen it last, and he saw nothing — no flag, no leader. He looked around and suddenly, the flag appeared in the West. Whoops, wrong way, about face. The next day, he was ready to head West, when suddenly, there was no flag, no leader. Oh, there it was, facing South. But it was a different flag and a different leader. After a while, he said the leader and his flag disappeared completely, or he stopped following. He just found what seemed like a safe bunker and hunkered down hoping to survive. He counts four more years until retirement.

He finally opted for a voluntary layoff during the next reorganization. He said that he would prefer a strong leader with vision going in the wrong direction than no direction at all.

Visions Apply to People, Too

Visions apply to people, too. What vision do you have of your employees? Do you see your team as seriously lacking? Do you secretly wonder if any of them are really capable? Or do you see your team as superstars — capable and inspired? Your vision of your staff is important to the success of your total vision.

One organization asked for some help in closing the gap between the front-line supervisors and the rest of the management group. For many reasons, a fundamental difference existed between the front-line supervisors and other levels of management. Closing gaps could require a great deal of time and effort. Therefore, the first step the management group tackled was to decide if all the front-line supervisors were "able to respond to development and become members of the management team."

With these criteria in mind, the managers decided if each supervisor could be developed. Nearly 70 percent of the front-line supervisors were "questionable." I don't know what the correct percentage should be, but it seems to me that 70 percent is high. This plant is a world leader in the manufacturing of its product. How could 70 percent of the front-line supervisors be "questionable?" What seemed obvious to me was that this group of managers had no vision of success for their front-line supervisors.

What about the front-line supervisors? What vision did they think the managers had of them? I heard the following when I interviewed them: "They think we are a bunch of dummies. They don't value our experience. They try to tell us what to do and how to do it, yet they never ask our opinion. They don't give us credit for having a brain."

Was the vision clear for the front-line supervisors? You bet. They had gotten the message that they were "questionable" — or worse.

The story above illustrates a vision problem with an entire group. Much more frequently we encounter vision problems with individual performers. Admittedly, some people just cannot or will not perform the job. However, sometimes our "performance problems" reflect our vision of the person performing the job. We have no vision of his success, only a vision that he can't or won't succeed.

On the other hand, Jenna shows us how her positive vision of people's abilities served her, the people, and the organization quite well.

Jenna had a tough job. The government bureaucracy in which she worked was filled with complicated jargon and forms. Yet, her customers were ordinary people. People who really didn't know or care to know the difference between an FR385 and an 865F addendum. Besides, shouldn't the government take care of this stuff? Why is it that the government makes these rules and regulations so complicated, then scoffs at the customer when the customer doesn't have the right form or paperwork to get the job done? Well, Jenna decided to do something to improve this jargony, regulated world for her customers. She decided to take her staff of ordinary government clerks and teach them to become competent public speakers who could explain this complicated world in easy-to-understand language.

Most of her staff thought, "No way. We could never feel comfortable speaking in public."

Jenna persisted. She didn't force anyone, but she asked for volunteers for her speaking team. Only two people came forward and said they would be willing to give it a try. Jenna made the team sessions fun. She rewarded first attempts with prizes and certificates and balloons. She used squirt guns and buzzers for any hints of self-doubt. Soon, the two were joined by two more. Then two more. Then a final group of three joined the crowd.

Nine competent public speakers emerged from this group of "ordinary government clerks." Why? Because Jenna insisted not that they do it, but that they could do it. She believed in them. Her positive vision allowed them to succeed.

The team was recognized by the organization's president. Members received a cash bonus for their accomplishments and wonderful congratulatory remarks.

Beyond the walls of home, these clerks presented their team achievements at a national conference on team accomplishments. Also, they became a model for other organizations wanting to implement similar initiatives.

But none of this compares to the feelings these people have about their own achievement. "I never thought I could do this. It's surprising to me that our boss believed in us more than we believed in ourselves. I never thought I could get up in front of 200 people and hold their attention, let alone get a few laughs. It feels so good."

You cannot dismiss the power of having vision for your mission and the people who will carry it out. Either can have dramatic influence on your success as a leader.

Communicating Vision Clearly

To convince requires belief.

If you can't believe the vision, don't try to convince others. The leader's all-consuming commitment to the vision is essential and obvious to everyone. There is no room for a half-hearted attempt. Either commit or forget. Commitment is impossible to feign, yet without it, the leader will surely fail.

Once you have your heart right, you must communicate the vision to the people surrounding you. Clearly articulating the pictures, the new version of reality, is at the very heart of leadership. Thus far, this is the first step in a journey that from this point forward, involves other people. Inspiring others toward the dream begins with this first step.

Because the best vision comes from the heart and the mind, communicating the vision from that special place is the key to adding vitality to the vision. Choose word pictures that inspire and engage the heart. Visions are important to get the mind thinking, but equally if not more important, visions should stir something much greater than thought. If visions are the stuff of dreams, then the words used to communicate them must be the words of the spirit.

Remember Kristine's words as she spoke about the patients. She wanted her staff to think about "pampering important, deeply loved guests who felt ill and were visiting the staff's home." She didn't say "we would like to improve the quality of patient care during the admission process." That's trite, it's boring, and it doesn't provoke an emotional response or connection to the vision.

Unfortunately, sometimes leaders just don't understand how important this step is. This is hard work and it isn't accomplished in just one attempt. Communicating vision is a constant job on the "things to do" list. It can't ever afford to take a back seat. Instead, every action, every decision, every question, should link to the vision. The leader should always be asking: How is this tied to our vision? How does this affect our vision? How does this pamper our dearly loved important guests who are visiting today?

This reminds me of an intelligent leader of an organization of about 3500 employees. He had a clear vision that involved changing the culture of this organization to increase employee participation in decisions affecting the customer and quality. This man's vision was clear. He knew and could articulate this vision quite well. If asked, he could describe this organization of the future. He told a few of his senior leaders about his vision. And that is the end of the story! He didn't tell anyone else. He didn't retell and retell his vision. He didn't make his vision a part of every action and decision. He didn't question how actions tie into the vision. Two years later, he couldn't understand why his vision hadn't taken root.

Visions are fragile creations. They can quickly be smashed or smothered by the daily routine of doing business. It is difficult to penetrate the imprisoning walls of the status quo. Leading means constantly mentoring all others to see the vision, never letting an opportunity pass to restate the vision. The leader is always looking for exceptions to the vision, not to punish, but to teach the vision repeatedly. As repetition is the key to learning, it is also the key to visioning. The leader cannot drop the vision. She cannot write it at a corporate retreat and put it in the drawer. All day, every day, the vision must be in front of the leader — and the leader must keep it in front of all others. It takes at least two to five years to incubate a vision.

From Leader to Leader – Passing Vision

Passing vision from leader to leader
is like passing a flickering candle in a windstorm.

Most of the time you are not the sole creator of vision within your organization. More often than not, you have someone's vision that you must blend with your own. The company president, your division manager, or your board of directors also has a vision and frankly, that is a very important fact. You can create a vision for your department or section or plant, but your vision probably must tie to some larger vision.

As a leader caught somewhere in the middle, you need to develop the skill of understanding vision so you can pass it along in the spirit in which it was intended. Too often, leaders throughout the organization confuse, distort, over-complicate, or ignore the vision. Shame on them.

But shame on you, too, if you don't take the time to understand the vision of others and how you blend it with your own. The most important skill in understanding another's vision is listening. You must listen intently and actively to learn what your leader sees. Ask questions, seek advice, discuss and argue until you finally understand. Then, and only then, can you articulate it to the people you lead. Also, after you have a thorough understanding, you can weave your vision in and around that of the leader.

You will be faced with a major problem if you can't believe in the vision of your leader. If this situation arises, you can no longer be effective. You will become the proverbial roadblock. Either get out of the way, or find a way to believe. The choice is yours at first. Later, you may not have a choice.

Suppose you choose to believe the vision of your leader; you now have an exciting opportunity. You can now create your own vision within the vision. What can you see your section or department becoming? One by one you can touch the lives of each person in your section or department and place within their hearts this vision of the future — engaging their minds, their bodies, and their souls in its creation.

Spirit Killers and Soul Suckers

INCONGRUENT ACTIONS

If you were going to build your dream home, you wouldn't set the foundation in a base of quicksand. Yet, leaders do this all the time. That's why directions shift from day to day, actions differ from words. These leaders' visions have no firm base. If you canvass the halls of any organization, you can find many examples of this problem. If you listen closely to what people say about this, you will find that it leaves permanent scars in the form of dampened spirits.

The organizational cynics have turned this into a hobby. They pass time by keeping careful watch for incongruent actions of their leaders and they keep score by counting the hash marks on the spirits of their coworkers.

NO ACTION

As common as incongruent actions are leaders who state grand vision and then take little or no action to get there. "This too shall pass" becomes the war cry of the troops who have wearily traveled this road before. It is hard to take vision statements seriously when, so often, little or nothing follows. Leaders need to act on their vision, and they need to act in a reasonable amount of time. The longer the vision goes without supporting action, the greater the likelihood that it will fizzle and die.

When we talked about vision, one group of managers rolled their eyes and said, "Oh we have great vision. Vision isn't our problem. We don't have action."

They relayed a story of a gallant effort to overhaul an area of the company that was – and had been for some time – a serious problem. After rounding up the best minds in the company and investing several months, the group put together a plan that everyone agreed would be a tremendous improvement for the company. However, the plan called for some tough actions, including dramatically reducing the number of management and support staff.

When the group finished its work and presented its recommendations to the president, the members expected that at least some portion of the plan if not all of it, would be implemented immediately. What resulted was absolutely nothing. Management ignored their recommendations. Never again were the works of this group mentioned and neither was the problem. Talk about a spirit killer.

OVER-COMPLICATING THE VISION

Sometimes leaders state visions that are so complicated we can barely read them, let alone remember them. If people can't remember the vision, chances are it isn't simple enough.

Another problem is that often leaders somewhere in the middle take a simple vision and transform it into a nightmarish bureaucracy.

Keep it simple. If you don't, by the time it gets to the bottom, no one is going to understand it and they can't possibly carry it out.

SABOTAGING VISION

Some — often only a few — people in the organization know the vision and understand it, but work in exactly the opposite direction. They deliberately sabotage the vision. Other people in the organization know who is sabotaging and they expect that the leadership does, as well. If nothing is done to stop these efforts, then those who are putting forth genuine effort think, "What's the use?"

LOST IN THE DETAIL

Some managers are so detail-oriented that they simply can't understand the idea of vision. Minutia consume their attention and blur the "big picture." They can't imagine there is a tomorrow they should be thinking about in a creative way.

Don't misunderstand, details in any business or organization are critical. In fact, many times the reason visions fail is that no one is minding the details. However, the details need to be connected to the big picture. The leader's job is to help everyone attend to the proper details. In this way, the vision will become the new reality.

Dear Mr. Manager

I'm confused. I thought you hired me to bring new business to this company. I believe your words were, "Everyone in this company needs to understand that we can't survive without growth and new markets." I've been on the front line every day trying my best to live that vision for this company.

Yesterday, when I got the Monroe contract, you said that Jack threw a fit at the production meeting because no one told him we were trying to expand. Excuse me, but wasn't that the reason I was hired? And wasn't it your job to tell Jack what the plan was? We do not seem to have the same marching orders around here. Don't you think it's only fair for Jack and me to understand the same picture?

Respectfully,

Mr. Salesman

Dear Ms. Supervisor,

I went to the employee meeting yesterday and heard that management would like for us to give more ideas and suggestions for improvement. They said they value our ideas and need us to come to work and think about problems, potential problems, and ways to be more cost effective and quality conscience.

What caught my attention was the example they used. They said that all of Line II will need to be down for maintenance because no one said anything about a faulty cable. If someone had noticed or said something, his problem could have been avoided without shutting down the line.

Well, Ms. Supervisor, that's when I blew up. I told you two weeks ago about that cable. I told you Thursday morning and Friday afternoon. I even said that if someone doesn't fix this soon, it's going to cause the entire line to be shut down.

I'm tired of hearing one thing from senior management and another thing from you. Senior management says they value our ideas. Is that just empty rhetoric or is it true? If it's true, then I suggest you get with the program. If it isn't true, then just keep lying and covering your butt.

Bill

Every time a man puts a new idea across

he finds ten men who thought of it before he did —

but they only thought of it.

Anonymous

6. FUELING THE VISION

Energy and Vision

Shoes made completely of see-though plastic ... I remember when I was a child I had a vivid idea of clear plastic shoes. Years later, when Jellies stormed the market, I recall looking in amazement at this familiar image that I had conjured up in my mind more than twenty years before. Since then, sales of Jellies have exceeded the two billion mark.

You've done it, too. Can you recall walking through the shopping mall, flipping through a newspaper or magazine, or turning on the TV and suddenly finding yourself intrigued by the familiarity of some new product or idea? You think to yourself, "That's my idea, I thought of it first." Sure enough, you did. Well, that's great. Those ideas are the seeds of vision. As you develop these pictures even further, you become skilled at painting the future. Vision is essential for every leader.

But having great vision won't even buy you a cup of coffee. I haven't earned a dime from my clear-plastic shoe idea. What about you? Visions are critical to success, but they are no more than empty thoughts. In order to make a vision become reality, you must add energy. You must energize that vision every day of the year. It won't be enough to work at it now and then. Primarily, the leader must be the source of that energy.

Hal is one of the best leaders I know. He is a great leader for many reasons, but the gift he consistently gives is his energy toward a vision. Once he commits to a direction, this man and his team will no doubt succeed.

Hal heads one of four offices in an organization of about 1500 people. The president of this business wisely decided to embark on a quality initiative. He shared his vision with the four office heads. He allowed each office freedom to act on this vision and often expressed his commitment and encouraged each leader to "grow" the vision.

Three years later, the office Hal led was far ahead of the remaining offices on the road to quality. Why? Because every day for those three years, Hal had done something to further the vision. He went into the departments and had roundtable discussions about quality. He provided his management team with unending training on quality. He had meetings in which he asked each manager how the quality effort was progressing in her area. When a manager was stuck, he provided counsel and advice on how to get unstuck. Then he asked again about progress. He held a "Quality Fest" to nurture enthusiasm for quality. He launched teams on quality concerns. He rewarded team efforts. He made resources, both financial and human, available to further the vision. He acted. And acted. And acted. He got many people involved, but he knew the task of fueling the vision was too important to delegate.

Any question where this leader stood on quality? Not one. Why? Because every day, he fueled the vision with his energy.

Once the leader commits himself and his energy toward a vision, the next task is to harness the energy of everyone else in the corporation toward this vision. Look around your place of work. People everywhere are expending energy. People come to work every day and accomplish something. The challenge of leadership is to ensure that people are doing the "right" somethings. The right somethings are the ones that fuel the vision.

Often we see well-intentioned employees working hard and expending energy, but that energy is not focused on things that can move the organization closer to the vision. It's like the great fifty-yard football play toward the wrong goal-post. At least, you have the crowd screaming, "No! No! Wrong direction!"

It's the leader's job to shout, "No! No! Wrong direction!" The leader must look for the well-intentioned who are going in the wrong direction. Then, he must help them see the right direction. A group of adjustment clerks at a financial institution expressed it like this.

"Our department's job is to correct errors on financial statements. The errors result from processing mistakes made by our operation's department. The number of backlog items is the measure for our department's performance and our individual performance — the higher the backlog, the lower our performance. Our manager kept careful watch on the measure, and he kept pushing harder and harder. He wanted us to do more adjustments to reduce the backlog. We worked mandatory overtime five days a week and worked Saturdays to reduce the backlog. No matter how long or hard we worked, it didn't seem to make a dent in our backlog numbers. We were burned out.

"A new manager looked at the situation and agreed that backlog was an important measure for our unit. But he redirected our energy. Instead of requiring us to work overtime to process adjustments, he required us to apply our knowledge of errors to help the operation's department make fewer mistakes. Not only did this reduce our backlog, it also made our customers much happier. The good news for us is that we are now able to enjoy our families at 5 P.M.

"The clerks formed a team consisting of people from all areas of operations. They collected data on errors, researched causes, implemented solutions, and tracked results. Leaders provided information and support *and* the vision for the team. The vision was harmoniously working together to achieve error-free processing. The numeric result: the backlog was reduced by 87% and remained at this low level. The human result: elation, soaring spirits, pride, and confidence."

This leader harnessed and directed the energy of the many. The smart leader taps the creativity of the people and directs this creativity toward the vision. If they know what the vision is, most people will work toward it. If given permission, most people will not only work toward it, they will enhance it. If you wonder why some leaders are so successful at getting things done, watch where their energy goes. And watch where they direct the energy of others.

In organizations plagued by wave after wave of downsizing, we see high levels of energy expended on fear, resentment, and worry as employees wonder if they are next in line to be shoved out the door. The leader who charts a clear direction, even in the face of uncertainty, focuses the energy of those remaining. He may not be able to take away the fear, but he can and must show the intended path. Sadly, in these situations when leadership can make an important difference, the leaders are painfully lacking.

Brian works for an organization that was downsized three times in the last three years. In a department that once had 21 persons, Brian and 2 co-workers now carry the entire burden.

"In the past, I felt insecure about my job, but now I also worry about my job performance. There is just no way we can do it all. Things are falling through the cracks. Every day I go home exhausted and worried that I missed something important. My boss only makes matters worse. The other day he complained that we missed sending a monthly report to headquarters. Meanwhile, he was the one who told us to stop creating the report. He said if they missed it they would ask for it. Well, they asked for it. Instead of taking the heat and telling them that with limited resources, he decided the report wasn't necessary, he turned around and blamed us. There are only so many hours in the day. We can't do everything. Someone has to take responsibility to say what is important. Where do you want us to spend our energy?"

Top Ten Vision Killers
—or—
How to Kill a Vision Without Even Trying

Nearly one thousand responses from employees of all levels and professions clearly identified these top ten vision killers:

Leaders kill a vision by:

1. Treating people badly, such as, not showing people they care, forgetting to say thank you, not respecting people, not making people feel valued.

2. Not setting good examples, living by the adage "Do as I say, not as I do."

3. Focusing on too many things at once.

4. Pushing too hard on the task and forgetting the people.

5. Not giving clear direction.

6. Giving inconsistent direction.

7. Not taking responsibility for failure.

8. Focusing on the details and not telling the "why's" or the big picture.

9. Showing no personal commitment to the vision.

10. Allowing people who aren't performing the job to remain.

The Treasure in Passion

Passion for work is passion for life.

Can you imagine a symphony conductor without passion for music, a football coach without passion for the game, an artist without passion for his canvas? What about you? Do you have passion for making widgets? I've lost you? What is exciting about creating widgets?

Most of us spend at least a third of our time each day at work. I hear you saying that the average worker just doesn't care. He wants to put in his eight hours and go home. I suggest that there aren't many typists out there who want to create a page with a mistake, not many pipe fitters who want to fix it with a "leak," and not many machine operators who want to push the wrong buttons.

I suggest that part of the apathy — and the resultant lack of energy — you see comes from the lack of passion and caring these workers see in their co-workers, their leaders, and their organization.

That perception and that trend are what you must stop. The first "baby step" toward breaking that trend is for you to walk through the door each day with your soul and your spirit in hand and a driving passion for fueling the vision.

But you say that isn't possible, that you are not in a high enough position to change your organization. In my many interviews with everyday workers, I heard repeatedly that you can and you do make a difference. That the person who is "in charge" of the section or group is the person who sets the tone.

I had an interesting conversation with "Stone," a pipe fitter who was at least 6'6" and 300 pounds and had serpent tattoos covering both forearms. He had been with this company for more than fifteen years. His job performance was erratic. Sometimes Stone performed like a star. At other times, Stone just didn't seem to care. However, he was considered one of the most skilled pipe fitters the company had. Some of the work was highly complex and very involved in hydraulic systems and vacuum systems.

I asked him when he felt inclined to do his best work. His instant reply was, "when the bastards who are supposed to be the leaders act like they give a damn!" He was speaking, of course, about management.

"Can you give me some examples?" I asked. He listed several supervisors he had worked for over the past several years.

"John, that bastard, I wouldn't give him anything, because he wouldn't give anything. He was so fuckin' lazy and he didn't give a damn about this place — so I figured, if he don't, I don't!"

As he went down the list, he eventually got to Mark.

"I'd do anything for that son-of-a-bitch," Stone said. "He was a good man. He cared about us. He drove us hard, but he drove himself hard, too. He cared about this company."

You can argue with Stone's logic. If he were internally motivated, it shouldn't matter what the boss brings to the job. Where is his sense of pride? I agree to some extent, but what about you? Don't you find it easier to do your best when the person leading you is also doing her best and caring about the job and about you?

And what if it seems as though no amount of passion is going to make much difference?

Consider Jim. Jim was a front-line supervisor in a government bureaucracy. This bureaucracy was so well established that it may have been the inventor of bureaucracy. People labored over endless paperwork, much of which seemed useless. They lived in a world of "i" dotting and "t" crossing. It was difficult, if not impossible, to make any impact on the people or the system. To top it off, they lived under constant scrutiny by the media. But for more than 30 years, Jim came to work each day and focused his group on the task at hand. His motto was "making a difference today by doing the best we can." For 30 years, he repeated this vision for his workers.

He knew what he could change — very little. He kept his crew focused on the positive contributions they could make, and he was there to support his staff through the rest of it. At his retirement dinner, people inside and outside the organization spoke about how he kept the passion burning. Every day his goal was to make a difference. He came to work to do his best and to help others do their best.

Jim never instituted any widespread or sweeping changes. Not many changes occurred over his 20 or 30 years. If anything was different, the organization was mired down in more bureaucracy. Sometimes, leadership, especially for the front line or even middle layers, isn't about sweeping visions of change. It is about bringing passion to the mundane. It is easy to feel passionate about ideas or visions you helped create. It is much more difficult to bring passion to a workplace in which you must accept things that are much less than or different from what you would like. Some would say that you could leave, and you could, but sometimes financial realities or other realities make that choice riskier than is acceptable. What, then? You can choose to be negative and stay trapped in a terrible system, or you can adopt Jim's vision. You can choose to bring your spirit to work every day and invite others to do the same.

One of the greatest gifts a leader can bring is passion for the vision. Passion is exciting; passion is energizing; passion is contagious. Passion and deep caring about the vision, the job to be done, and ultimately, the people doing the job, are the seeds of inspiration. If you have ever had the pleasure of working for someone who passionately believes in what he is doing, you know how this feels.

Advice from Employees on Fueling the Vision

This generous advice on how to fuel vision comes from nearly 1000 interviews from people at all levels of the organization:

1. Believe it yourself. Don't give us a line of bull. We know when you are telling us the truth and when you are handing us a line.

2. Ask us how to make it work. Don't just tell us what to do. We have a brain. Ask us what we think.

3. Lovingly shout, "No, no! Wrong direction!" Don't expect us to know if you haven't told us. Don't ridicule or belittle us.

4. Set the example. Don't tell us that customers are the No. 1 priority and then blow them off or call them assholes when they leave.

5. Act like you give a damn. Don't expect us to care when you don't care about this place, this job, or our customers.

6. Direct and focus our energy in the same direction simultaneously. We hate it when you tell Susan to do something

and then give the same assignment to Jeff. We should be working together. That's demeaning and we feel like it is a waste of our time. Is this a contest or what?

7. Deal with the people who aren't doing the job. Don't ask us to do more when they aren't carrying their share of the load. That's unfair.

8. Don't give us inconsistent messages. Don't tell us one minute to do something and then turn around and tell us the opposite the next minute. We're not stupid.

9. Ask us what is going wrong. When we're not meeting our goals, there is usually a reason. We probably know what it is. Ask us.

10. Take responsibility for failures. Don't leave us out to dry. Have the courage to tell them it was everyone's mistake, including yours.

11. Give us the big picture. You don't tell us why or how things fit together. Give us the big picture and then hold us accountable for making the right decisions.

12. Believe in us. Believe that we can deliver. Believe that we can make good judgments. We can. We will come through.

Spirit Killers and Soul Suckers

OUTWARD INERTIA

If you can't move yourself, you can't move others. You must be able to mobilize your own energy in the direction of your vision. Some people see the vision, can articulate the vision, but fail to take steps toward the vision.

Sally was the founder of a small wholesale company. She had good vision for her company. She believed in what she was trying to accomplish. She convinced the bankers that her vision was sound. Unfortunately, when Sally needed to take steps to move her company forward, she stopped dead in her tracks. Several key employees suggested how she might move forward, but her response was: "Well, I don't know, let me think about it." This constant inertia just dragged things to a halt.

Sure, all leaders are entitled to have occasional bouts of inaction. In fact, these periods may serve a purpose. But constant inertia kills vision. Only energy makes vision a reality.

LACK OF ENTHUSIASM

When you talk about your department or area and you sound like verbal ether, how can you expect enthusiasm from your employees? If you want to put fire in someone's gut, you'll need to provide the spark for the flame. Haven't got a spark? Then, find a spark, make a spark, set a fire. It's your job. If you can't find or make a spark, then get a new job.

LACK OF CONFIDENCE

If you don't have confidence in your vision and the path toward that vision, others will immediately sense this. If you don't, why should they?

I recall a company that committed a great deal of time and energy on a major workplace redesign. This company had union participation and support and everyone agreed that this was the "right" thing to do — everyone except one key supervisor.

When it was time to implement, this supervisor, who had participated in all the discussions and had the opportunity to shape the implementation, just wouldn't accept the fact that this was the right thing to do. He did go along with the program. Unfortunately, when it came to carrying it out, he just never put his heart into it. He didn't really believe in the vision, so it was nearly impossible for him to address objections and issues that came up on the floor.

It was so obvious that this person lacked confidence in the vision that the people he was leading instantly knew he wasn't committed. All of the other areas of the shop were doing very well in the redesign efforts. However, this one key area, led by this supervisor who lacked confidence in the vision, was in chaos.

FEAR

Perhaps all of the above spirit killers link to fear. Somehow, we are afraid to commit to our vision. We are afraid to speak too loudly in favor of our vision. Are we afraid it isn't right? Are we afraid others will criticize? Do we think someone will call it stupid? Are we afraid someone will laugh? Maybe so. But if we are afraid to speak up and embrace our vision with passion, it is ridiculous to expect others to work toward it with passion.

Dear Boss,

You don't believe in this place.
It's obvious. You struggle through your
day. I think you must feel completely
drained when you go home.
The problem though, is that if you
don't believe in what you are doing,
how can you expect us to?

Jane

Dear Supervisor,

You and I have had some differences through the years, but there is one thing that I really admire about you.

You really care about this place. You come in every day and give it 100%. It's hard not to give my best when I'm working beside you. I admire the fact that you leave your troubles at home and that you don't let things dampen your spirits here. You're kinda like the Energizer Bunny. You just keep on going.

Thanks boss. I appreciate the motivation. You challenge all of us to do more by the example that you set.

Sincerely,

Dee

The Third Key

BE REAL

INTRODUCTION

W HY IS SCOTT ADAMS'S DILBERT cartoon book one
of the best-selling management books ever written? Because it is
dreadfully true. Employees are hungry for authentic leaders who
know how to lead. More than 88% of interviewees said they know
leaders who play the role. They defined "playing the role," as both
power-hungry leaders who push others around so they can feel important, and wishy-washy leaders who wait to see which way the wind is
blowing before taking a stand.

Workers seek authentic, genuine, verifiable, bona fide, original
leaders. Not cardboard cutouts. You have no hope of ever being a
leader if you cannot be real. If you don't know who you are and what
you stand for, you aren't ready to be a leader.

Once you understand your values, your strengths and weak-
nesses, your core needs and motivations, and have used this information to develop your character, then you are on your way to becoming
authentic.

Discovery regarding power and the use and abuse of power also
contributes to the process of being real. The leader who has mastered
this important lesson serves his followers in a way that elevates their
spirits rather than diminishes them.

Above all, growth is continuous. The true leader never stops growing. She sets out a lifelong course for learning. The fruit at the end of the journey is a life of wisdom and honor — honor given away to others and honor received.

Life is like playing a violin in public

and learning the instrument

as one goes on.

Samuel Butler

7. KNOW THYSELF

Genuineness of Self

You've seen it. The images — the large corner office with windows sporting the best view of the city, the bookshelves proudly displaying the most current business best sellers, the artwork hand picked by the best interior designers, the Armani suits, the Rolex watch, not to mention the support staff — all point to the fact that this person is a leader. Right?

When the questions come, he always knows the right staff person to summon for the answers. (That's why you have staff, of course.) Then one day, a small voice interrupts with a rude and invasive question, "But you, sir, what do you think? What do you believe? What do you value?"

Suddenly stopped, realizing that he can't delegate this one, the speechless leader, like the deer caught in the headlight, stands paralyzed.

The role. We all know the leader who plays the role. He acts like others think he should act. He says what others think he should say. He may spend an inordinate amount of time learning to be a leader by reading all the latest management books, attending the best management seminars, and otherwise studying the role. He seeks role models and emulates their styles, their mannerisms, their likes and dislikes. This person may be well intentioned about the business of being a leader; however, something just doesn't fit.

This cardboard cutout leader must be introduced to someone special, someone who could help him in his career. Who? Who is this someone who could help so much with the business of leadership?

Himself.

Developing self, however, requires skill far beyond imitation. The true leader must discover the inner core or spirit that drives him. Touching this inner core allows the true leader freedom to be himself. No longer burdened by facade, the true leader knows the answer to the question, "But you, sir, what do you believe or value?" He understands beyond the books and the seminars, he understands from this core place that houses his unique fountain of wisdom. It is from this place alone that the leader defines himself. Here he learns who he is. When his actions are congruent with this being, then, and only then, he is genuine.

Genuineness requires diligent effort and demands that we explore our demons. By examining all of the shades of the soul's palette, we can get to know ourselves. Looking only at the pastel hues will paint a picture that may be pleasing, but the dark colors and shadows provide the depth. Being genuine asks us to be real. Margery Williams, in the children's classic The *Velveteen Rabbit*, captures the essence of real.

"Does it hurt to be real?" asks the Velveteen Rabbit to the Skin Horse.

"Sometimes," said the Skin Horse, for he was always truthful. "When you are Real you don't mind being hurt."

"Does it happen all at once, like being wound up," the Rabbit asked, "or bit by bit?" "It doesn't happen all at once," said the Skin Horse. "You become. It takes a long time. That's why it doesn't often happen to people who break easily, or have sharp edges, or who have to be carefully kept. Generally, by the time you are Real, most of your hair has been loved off, and your eyes drop out and you get loose in the joints and very shabby. But these things don't matter at all, because once you are Real you can't be ugly, except to people who don't understand."

From the Skin Horse, we learn that being real requires time. Time to capture the diary of our soul. Time to write the book that becomes our self. Time to sing the music that becomes the voice of our spirit. In time we are defined. And in time, we become. By taking the time to reflect on our experiences and our feelings, we develop our sense of values, our morality, our mystery, and our truth.

Exploring Core Leadership Values Related to Trust

Explore each of the core trust values — importance, touch, gratitude, and contributions — separately and reflect on the key learnings from each component. Consider the following from the perspective of being a follower. Then think about each question from the perspective of being a leader.

IMPORTANCE
As a follower:
Think about a time when someone:

Treated you like human equals.
Attached significance to the tasks you perform.
Attached importance to you in every interaction.
Worked each day to raise your dignity.
Recall as much as possible about the incident.
How did you feel?

As a leader:
Think about a time when you:

Treated someone as a human equal.
Attached significance to the tasks someone else performed.
Attached importance to someone else in your interaction.
Worked each day to raise someone else's dignity.
Recall as much as possible about the incident.
How did you feel?
How did it make others feel?

TOUCH
As a follower:
Think about a time when someone:

Honored you by listening with an open mind and heart.
Expressed genuine caring for you.
Created a "no blame" culture.
Expressed positive beliefs about you.
Recall as much as possible about the incident.
How did you feel?

As a leader:
Think about a time when you:

Honored someone by listening with an open mind and heart.

Expressed genuine caring for someone.

Created a "no blame" culture.

Expressed positive beliefs about someone on your staff.

Recall as much as possible about the incident.

How did you feel?

How did it make others feel?

GRATITUDE

As a follower:
Think about a time when someone:

Developed a grateful eye for you.

Felt genuinely grateful for your skills, behaviors, sacrifices, attitudes, and knowledge.

Wanted to elevate you through gratitude.

Expressed gratitude for something you did.

Recall as much as possible about the incident.

How did you feel?

As a leader:
Think about a time when you:

Developed a grateful eye for someone else.

Felt genuinely grateful for someone's skills, behaviors, sacrifices, attitudes, and knowledge.

Wanted to elevate someone else through gratitude.

Expressed gratitude for something someone else did.
Recall as much as possible about the incident.
How did you feel?
How did it make others feel?

CONTRIBUTIONS
As a follower:
Think about a time when:

You worked in an environment in which everything was equal and fair.

The leader's actions and reactions made the environment equal and fair.

A leader took a stand.

A leader expressed the important workplace values.

A leader faced an unpleasant truth with a gentle heart.

Recall as much as possible about the incident.

How did you feel?

As a leader:
Think about a time when you:

Worked in an environment in which everything was equal and fair.

Created an environment that was equal and fair.

Took a stand.

Expressed the important workplace values.

Faced an unpleasant truth with a gentle heart.

Recall as much as possible about the incident.

How did you feel?

How did it make others feel?

Interior Power and Leadership

*The best effect of fine persons
is felt after we have left their presence.*

Ralph Waldo Emerson

Power. Abuse of power, positional power, power mongers, power seekers, power hungry, power language, power dress, power play, power politics, power people, power talk, power everything! Ours is a society obsessed with the words and the deeds of power. We have it, lose it, need it, want it, abuse it.

Sadly, we've missed the true meaning of power. Power is not a thing to have, to abuse, to need, or to want. It is instead, something that flows from a well-cultivated self, a self that is assured and confident in its actions. Ultimately, it is the only true power anyone has.

When a leader has this interior power, it is obvious to those around him. People are drawn to it. This inner strength calls others like a magnet. Those around it feel the strength, the presence, and the confidence. Within this interior power are the true roots of leadership. Interior power is the source from which the leader will draw all other dimensions of leadership. It is from here that vision, direction, and inspiration are seeded.

We want leaders who know the way. If they don't know the way, we want leaders who are confident they can find the way. "Confident" doesn't mean the leader has all the answers. It simply means that he is committed and believes he can find the answers. This power allows him to take the risk necessary for gain.

Often hidden behind the loudest voices are leaders who lack interior power. The person who raises his voice to make a point, who shouts in anger, who manipulates, or who demands power is most often the one with the least inner strength. But compensating for what is lacking in strength by turning up the volume does not accomplish much. This immediate display of emotion may deliver short-term results, but it has little chance of delivering trust and inspiration, the stuff futures are made of.

Control also suggests a lack of interior power. People who need to control everything in their environment — the people, the events, the places — are most often insecure. They have a basic disbelief and distrust of self and others.

In one of my many interviews with Harry, he admitted being a control freak. He had to know exactly what everyone was doing, how they were doing it, when they were doing it, and he had to make sure that they did it his way. It was his way or no way. When I challenged him to lighten up a bit — to let people breathe and think for themselves — he cringed. Letting go, even a little bit just did not seem possible. When I pushed him for reasons, Harry said that he was a perfectionist and wanted things done right. As we delved deeper into this subject, Harry admitted that he was concerned about letting people down, that somehow, he would be found out. The company had placed all this respect and responsibility on him and maybe, just maybe, he didn't deserve it. Maybe he couldn't live up to it all. Maybe he wasn't worthy. So he tried to control everything because he didn't want to let anyone down. What a heavy, if not impossible, burden for any leader to carry.

One last beauty of interior power that is important for any leader: True interior power sparks power in others. It can be given away freely and will come back with great return. It is the essence of empowerment. Empowering means enabling others to do their jobs to the best of their ability. What better way to enable, than to help spark one's power — to give to others the permission to use their interior strength to accomplish the task at hand. For those whose interior power is dim, this is more than necessary; this is a true gift of leadership.

How strong is your sense of interior power?

Do you feel a need to control situations or people?

Would others see you as empowering?

Whom do you disempower? Why?

How can you strengthen your inner power?

A Process for Growth

Argue for your limitations, and sure enough, they're yours.
Richard Bach

The path to growth can take many different avenues, so the most important step is to get moving. Don't waste your time making excuses or feeding your limitations. Instead fight for what you can be, what you are destined to be. Feed the passions of your dreams.

This simple five-step model may help. It has helped me, but remember, the important thing is not to use my model, but to find a model that works for you — and that you *do* proceed.

1. Seek Comment

The true leader seeks truth. She invites it, makes a home for it, and encourages it to stay. She knows that through truth she will grow. Ask for comment on actions and words. Seek comments from critics and friends. Pay closest attention to that spoken by your greatest foe. The kernel of truth here may be the hardest to sow, yet could produce the most bountiful harvest.

2. Reflect

Take the comment inside for reflection. Reflection serves to brew, not filter, the truth; in time, the true flavor emerges. It is in the quiet moments of reflection that we face truth. But it is in these critical moments that we make choices. We can be strong and use the truth as a spring from which to grow and leap forward. We can be afraid and choose to ignore the truth. Or we can choose laziness and live with the status quo. Ultimately, if growth of the inner self is the ultimate goal, then only through seeking truth and reflecting on it will we grow new selves — fuller, richer, and deeper selves.

I recall a session following an assessment workshop in which I was supposed to comment on the strengths and weakness of participants. A particular young man told me that he wanted "the truth." Pull no punches, give it to me straight, don't cover it in fluff, he instructed me. So I began. Before I could finish my first sentence, he interrupted with a defensive explanation. I continued; then he interrupted again with more defensive explanations. I stopped. This young man in no way wanted "the truth." He wanted only his version of truth. Growth will be a long time in coming for this young man.

3. Study Past Lessons

How do things connect? What patterns do you see in your life? Leaders look for links among the past and the present and the future. Try to discover the similarities in your successes and your failures. Through this information, you will gain great insight into your needs.

When most people name the things in their lives that caused the most growth, very often, they talk about events in their lives that caused pain. Many people start by saying that although they wouldn't want to go back to that time or place, they surely did learn a great deal from these negative experiences.

What gains have you received from pain? How are you linking these gains to what you do every day? How has your pain defined who you are? What insights have you gained about yourself and others?

4. Picture You and Laugh

We ask that you develop your inner self with an eye toward merriment. Growth should be fun. Truth often sheds light on our shortcomings and mistakes as leaders. And you must admit sometimes our shortcomings and mistakes are downright hilarious. If we could just look from afar with a playful heart, we would see that we are at times, truly ridiculous. Sometimes, we are most ridiculous when trying to be the most serious. Step back, appreciate the humor of leadership. How often have you and your co-workers made fun of "the boss" once he's left the room? Why? Because, when people try to be the boss or anything else that they aren't, it can be funny. Read the comic section, watch the latest TV show, or go to the movies. These are filled with examples of ridiculing the absurdities of leadership. Where do you see yourself? Which cartoon character exemplifies your bumbling leadership style? Where can you laugh at yourself? The ability to laugh at our shortcomings and mistakes makes the spirit light. In lightness, we can dance to greater heights.

One day I finally saw myself rushing like the White Rabbit in *Alice in Wonderland*. My vision was complete with theme music, "You're late, you're late, you're late for an important date." When I told a friend about this he agreed adding, "Yeah, you're like the hummingbird of the human species." Finally, it dawned on me that I am always in this frenzied state and that I am the only one who has the power to change it.

On the positive side, I see myself as Wile E. Coyote, in that I am resilient and I do not give up. Even when obstacles or failures present, I dust myself off and look for the next opportunity to pursue the roadrunners.

I pasted these powerful images on the refrigerator door to serve as constant reminders of what I am and what I want to become. Besides that, they provide great comic relief.

5. Give Yourself Permission to Grow

For some, cultivating an inner self somehow requires permission. Some people aren't even sure if it is OK. Maybe we learned that leanings in this direction are selfish; or maybe we learned not to think for ourselves; maybe we don't know if it is the right thing to do; or perhaps, it is just within our personalities to be hesitant about things. Free yourself, give yourself permission to learn and to explore the innermost expression of you. It is from here that the true leader will emerge.

Spirit Killers and Soul Suckers

CELEBRITY EGO

Everyone knows someone whose "EGO" is too big. Egotism is a major spirit killer. It's our egotism that holds us back from learning more about ourselves. If we already believe that we are great, then why would we consider changing? This blocks us from listening to the truth — and the bigger the "EGO," the larger the block. If we would just drop the celebrity status and work to be real, then we just might grow. Interestingly, leaders sometime adopt this celebrity status because they really don't know any other way to be. They are playing the "role" that we mentioned earlier and somewhere along the line, they picked up the notion of acting "big."

I don't need to tell you that besides blocking the growth of the leader, this is a major turnoff to those around him. If you want to see something interesting, watch the body language of the people responding to this "big" person. The celebrity EGO also rears its ugly head in terms of power. Most people who have a need to display power are coming from this position; these people use power in all its baseness.

FEAR

The greatest demon lurking to steal and stifle our interior power is fear. Fear abounds in degrees and levels that are unfathomable. The problem is that we give it free reign over our spirits and our hearts, allowing it the privilege to sap and suck our energy. Fear of rejection, fear of making a mistake, fear of retribution, fear of others, fear of self — these fears become our chorus. If one is unable to sing, another steps in, sometimes merging their voices in endless cacophony.

If we can't find a way to manage this fear, it overcomes and paralyzes us. We need to believe we can and do have control over it. We need to stop being afraid. If we don't stop, we will never grow.

BULLYING

As if we can't generate enough fear on our own, insensitive, insecure tyrants add to our fear through intimidation and bullying tactics. These masters of vile invade — with our permission — our inner selves, killing precious pieces of soul. They browbeat us into submission, arm wrestle until we say "uncle." We just resign because we really don't have the strength to fight anymore.

I was once interviewing a very confident leader on the subject of empowerment. Al was a perfect role model of someone who felt empowered. He was not afraid to take risks. He was confident and generally just a very strong individual. It was hard for me to imagine that he could ever feel disempowered. So I asked him if there were ever a time when he did.

He thought for some time over a very long career, during which time he had worked for many different types of bosses. Only once did he feel truly disempowered, when he worked for an absolute bully of a boss. The boss controlled everything. Al worked for this man for more than a year. During this time, the bully ridiculed and criticized every bit of Al's work.

On one of Al's project, his boss had literally combed through every word until finally he had agreed on the final effort. Al sent it to the printers to be completed just in time for the deadline. When his boss saw the final copy, he went into a screaming rage in front of the entire department over the cover page color. This empowered leader told me he felt reduced to nothing, totally disempowered to do any part of his job. That incident convinced him that he had to leave the department. Within a month he had another job.

LAZINESS

Lazy seeks the easy way. Growth is not easy. It requires intro-spection and reflection on some difficult subject matter. Then, it requires us to change. It is easier not to change. If we let laziness win, perhaps our life will be easy, but it will also be stagnant.

INNER INERTIA

Sometimes people do all the right things to develop themselves. They reflect, see truth, see the required change. Perhaps they even begin the difficult journey of change. Then, they get stuck and stay stuck. After that, they just hang in a state of limbo. They can't pry themselves loose. They're just like a cat stuck in a tree, only there's no fire department to call.

IGNORING TRUTH

We have honed our ability to ignore truth. We hear it, but we readily reject it as untruth. We find reason to dismiss it quickly and painlessly, before it can enter and be considered in any depth.

Dear Ms. Manager,

When are you going to drop the mask?
The other day, I thought I saw a
glimpse of you. You let your guard down
just for a moment and you acted like
one of us. You laughed with us. I was
amazed. Why can't you be that way every
day? Why do you insist on acting like
the boss? If you would just be
yourself, you might actually be OK. Are
you worried that if you get too close
we won't respect you? That isn't true.
I am not talking about becoming best
friends. I just think you should
lighten up. I think we could get the
same amount of work done, maybe more,
if you just stopped acting like the
boss. It's not that you are a tyrant,
it's that you just won't allow yourself
to feel comfortable around us.

Just be yourself.

Dear Ass Kicker,

When are you going to get off your power trip?

You are so absurd. You haven't figured out that the harder you kick, the weaker you look. You do seem to get some pleasure out of trying to make the rest of us look small. The problem is, you are the one who is shrinking every time you abuse your power.

The most powerful person that I ever met never raised his voice. His power came from respect. He earned it every day because of the character that he had developed. You have a long way to go to gain our respect.

Grow up. Look at how stupid you look.

Maryann

SPIRALING

UPWARD

INTRODUCTION

Few people feel inspired at work on any regular basis. In fact, most see themselves as underutilized. Underutilized meant that their ideas, thoughts, and creativity were not tapped. Underutilized did not mean under worked. Most workers did see themselves as busy, overloaded, and overwhelmed by the sheer volume of work they had to do, thus leaving little or no time for creative thinking or long-term problem solving.

- ❖ 85% of workers said they were underutilized at work

- ❖ 78% rarely or never think about long-term problem solving or creative ideas as it applies to work because there is simply no time for such activities.

What an incredible waste of human resources. The leader committed to finding the key to this treasure chest is sure to find the gold. The gold, however, may surprise you.

The leader called to spark inspiration is called to a higher path. This leader understands the limitations of motivation and rewards. He knows intrinsically that inspired performance does not result because of a monetary reward at the end of the stick.

So just what is this mystery that sparks inspiration?

To inspire —

1. to infuse an animating, quickening, or exalting influence into

2. to produce or arouse a feeling or thought

3. to affect with a specified feeling or thought

8. INSPIRATION

Inspiration and Inspired Leaders

Enlightened leaders understand the difference between motivation and inspiration, and they make it their goal to inspire their followers, not to simply motivate them. Inspiration is aimed at producing a feeling, thought, or action. Motivation is aimed at producing a desired behavior. Inspiration calls for breaking through to a point beyond where traditional models of motivation take us.

Depending on the circumstances and the rewards and punishments in place, most anyone can be motivated to change her behavior. Motivation is something that you do *to* someone. I can motivate my dog. (Fred will do just about anything for a biscuit.) But leaders quickly find the limitations of motivation in the workplace. After all, what rewards are truly big enough to make an impact on behavior? How many pizza parties can we have to celebrate a good safety record? And will a piece of pizza really motivate people to change their behavior? Probably not, but it is still a nice thing to do. Motivation, though, calls for a change in behavior. And at times, a change in behavior is the best that you can hope for. In fact, it would be a welcome relief to the current circumstance. Realistically, if we get that far with some people, we will have achieved something notable. However, inspiration calls for so much more.

Inspiration requires the leader to reach within the worker and find something fresh and worthy. Inspiration helps people say, "I can, I will, I want to, I must." Inspiration helps workers believe in themselves and say, "I have something really special here, and I will bring it forth in a way that only I can." To reach that breakthrough, the leader must touch workers to help shape their thoughts. It is through touch that the leader shapes the thoughts that change the way people think about themselves.

In this simple example, a manager took the time and touched Jimmy, a janitor at a local plant.

Jimmy worked second shift for a small glass manufacturer as a janitor. Since Jimmy had been hired, the floors shined, the trash was always emptied, and the bathrooms even smelled good. In fact, Jimmy made it a point to come in and ask the daylight people working in the factory if anything needed his special attention.

Marge, one of the managers at the company who often found herself working late, began to have brief talks with Jimmy about his plans and his future. Jimmy told her that he was a high school dropout and he couldn't read very well. Marge took the time to get the phone number of the local Adult Basic Education Center and General Educational Development (GED) office. She talked with Jimmy and encouraged him to give it a try.

At first, he resisted the idea. He said he didn't think he could ever be good at school stuff. After several

conversations, she finally convinced him that he had nothing to lose. In fact, she called the local Center and
arranged a meeting between a counselor and Jimmy. It
took nearly four years of hard work to overcome his reading disability, but Jimmy persisted and earned his GED.
Three years later, Jimmy graduated with an associate
degree from a local community college. Jimmy was promoted to computer operator with the company and refers
to Marge as his "inspiration."

However, it takes a secure and confident leader to inspire others.
Sadly, I've seen leaders who aren't confident about themselves or their
own position within the company and, therefore, simply can't find it
within themselves to inspire others.

Mary Beth had heard from several customers that
they were considering doing business elsewhere because
of slow response time on orders. She went to her boss with
a proposal that she was excited about. She had spent the
past four evenings working out the details of a plan she
thought could turn around response time. However, the
plan included a rather dramatic shift in the workforce and
schedules. After listening to the plan, the manager
responded by saying that the plan would draw attention
to a problem that might not even exist. He said he preferred keeping the department in a low profile. He also
thought that some people might be upset about the sched-

ule changes and they might complain to others in the company. He said that if he would propose such a plan, people would start asking questions. He told Mary Beth to keep working harder to satisfy the customers and that everything would probably work out. He did not encourage her plan, or even recognize her effort. Mary Beth left the meeting feeling dispirited and dejected.

This doesn't mean to imply that leaders should encourage workers carte blanche regardless of what they are proposing, but the seeds of inspiration will often either sprout or die depending on the nurturing they get from the leader. The leader's role is to develop the person and the idea for the good of the company. What might have happened to Mary Beth's idea and the company's progress had her manager reacted differently? We really don't know. But therein lies the problem: we can't see the great accomplishments that may lie ahead if the seeds of inspiration are not allowed to grow.

Occasionally, when the leader truly touches and inspires people, the result surprises the person as well as the leader.

Darla worked for a graphic arts company preparing graphics for multimedia presentations. Her boss saw great potential in her work and inspired her to higher and higher levels. Through her boss's coaching and caring, Darla had won several design awards and had developed a reputation for creativity and excellence in her field. She was a definite asset to the company.

But Darla often talked about another love. Her true love was oil painting. She talked to her boss about this, as well. True to his nature, he encouraged her to pursue what she loved. Darla and her boss had many discussions about vocation and avocation, and although her job allowed her to use many of her natural artistic gifts, it wasn't exactly what she wanted to do. She painted as a hobby for several years, but the voice kept nagging. Darla and her boss talked about life and a calling and the pursuit of one's goals.

One day Darla, with tears in her eyes, came in and thanked her boss for his inspiration and encouragement. She handed him her resignation and said that without him she couldn't have decided to leave the security of the company and open her own art studio.

Although Darla's leaving was quite a loss for the department, her boss felt genuinely pleased for her. Through the years, Darla's network and reputation in the art field grew. On many occasions, she recommended several people to her former place of employment — both potential customers and perspective employees.

Leaders who are characterized as inspiring are often inspired themselves. Their focus is clear, and they often give the impression that they know where they are going. They tend to be passionate about the journey. They also tend to recover from failure quickly rather than become paralyzed by it. The inspiration these leaders bring to the workplace tends to be contagious.

Walt worked for such a leader. At 7 a.m. each day, Pat was at the office and upbeat and ready for the challenges. She saw herself as a partner with her staff to overcome obstacles. She believed her staff could do anything, and she believed her job was to help them along the way.

One day, Walt was feeling particularly defeated on a software interface problem that was holding up the project the unit was working on. He entered her office feeling low. Pat immediately sensed his discomfort and listened as he explained that he had been working on this problem but seemed to be at a dead end. As he recounted his steps in solving the problem, he laced it with a large dose of self-flagellation.

Pat suddenly interrupted him with, "Walt, wait, stop. Listen to you. You are trying to convince me that you are an idiot. I'm sorry, but I know better. I'm not going to buy it. Look, you've come across a tough challenge. Look what you are letting it do to you. You are letting an intangible something ruin your self-esteem and confidence.

"Now come on, remember the time that Tom was stuck on the Ember project? What did we do? Did we conclude that Tom was an idiot? Of course not. We pulled together to figure out how to slay that dragon. Come on, it's OK to get stuck. It isn't OK to be miserable about it and not ask for help. Now, what can we do?"

Suddenly, Walt felt freed and renewed and hopeful — and a little foolish. Together, they pooled some help on the project and within two days they had a workable solution to the problem.

Inspiration may also require patience.

When Kelly talks about Sam, you can hear reverence in her voice. "He believed in me. He gave me a chance. I heard other people tell him that he was crazy, that I'd never be able to do it." Kelly explained. She spoke in a thick tongue and slurred speech resulting from brain damage that occurred at birth.

Kelly had been at this company for more than 10 years. In those 10 years she had missed work only two days. She was hired to deliver internal mail. All of the mail was sorted for her by floor. Her job consisted of riding the elevators in a large downtown office building and placing the mail for that floor in the designated spot. Kelly sometimes complained that she was bored. There had been a few attempts in the past to teach her some other basic tasks, but nothing ever seemed to work out. Everybody lost either their patience or their interest.

Unfortunately, things were changing. E-mail, faxes, and voice mail were making Kelly's job obsolete. Sam sat down with Kelly to talk to her about these changes. Kelly said that she understood. She said she realized that there wasn't as much mail as there used to be. She said she would be more than willing to do whatever Sam wanted her to do.

The majority of jobs in this building required either assembly skill, data entry, or clerical skills. None of these things seemed like a good match for Kelly, but Sam was willing to try. He asked her what job she thought she would like to do. Kelly selected an assembly job. Sam matched Kelly with the most patient person he could find and asked if she would train Kelly. This person agreed, but she was concerned about the task. Sam told Kelly and her trainer that he would do whatever it took to help them succeed. At the request of the trainer, Sam had some quick-reference guides designed especially for Kelly. Sam dodged a few sarcastic remarks and raised eyebrows, but he continued with the training plan.

The training period for this job was usually about a month. In this case, Sam patiently waited a full six months before Kelly was able to perform all of the job proficiencies. Throughout those six months, Sam stopped by every day to encourage Kelly. He also expressed his thanks to her trainer. Kelly was never at the top of the production list, but she was within the acceptable range of performance. However, her dedication and pride in her work and in herself were far above the acceptable range. For these qualities, Sam placed her on the top of the list.

The raised eyebrows and sarcastic remarks turned into applause when Kelly was voted by her peers as employee of the month.

Many leaders find themselves in mentoring roles. True mentoring encompasses all of the aspects of inspiration. Mentoring requires sharing and giving of oneself for the sake of helping another person. When someone in a leadership role mentors others, he willingly passes on all of the gifts and lessons he has gained over the years. Those gifts and lessons, when freely given, also seed inspiration.

The true power of inspired leadership lies in the feelings it can evoke in the followers. Inspiration renews and refreshes and changes the angle on the kaleidoscope, so that a whole new view is opened. Inspiration builds feelings of worth and self-esteem, so that a person can break through the barriers that hold him back.

The techniques for inspiration can't be listed on a do-and-don't list or any other list. Remember, inspiration is rooted in the leader's ability to touch, and there is no formula for touch. But time and again, people have told us that they felt most inspired by someone who believed in them, someone who helped them remove those ugly nagging doubts, or slay the dragons that held them captive. Inspiration removes the fear and propels people forward. Inspiration also makes people able to see things in a totally different perspective. Just when all views are exhausted, people become inspired because someone helps them see something in a different way. The leader's role is more that of a catalyst who serves to turn on the light. The leader who can inspire is truly enlightened.

In summary, we know that just by nature of title, some people will get things done. If we take that a step further and delegate tasks (tell people what to do), we will get further tasks accomplished. Over the years, we have learned that if we can improve the quality of our "telling" by delegating with clear expectations, our results should be even greater. Finally, we added the element of "coaching" and we learned that by stating our expectation and then by asking others how they can see this being accomplished, we will increase buy-in and increase our results even further. But we know that we can't possibly inspire people by telling them what to do. Telling will simply not bring inspiration. It may get results, but the true depth of what can be accomplished may never be known.

In order to inspire, a leader must first build trust. The building blocks that we've outlined in this book for building trust include: importance, touch, gratitude, and equitable contributions. From there, the leader must have vision and the energy to fuel the vision. Lastly, the leader must have intimate knowledge of self. With these gifts, the leader positions himself to inspire others.

Spirit Killer and Soul Suckers

FEAR

A leader cannot inspire others when he is crippled by his or her own fear. That's not to say that a leader must be fearless; in fact, it is better if the leader understands and has experienced fear and recognizes the power that it has to debilitate. This empathy will allow him or her to touch in the most genuine way. However, if the leader can't get past his or her own fear, then he or she may not have the confidence to help others get through their roadblocks.

JEALOUSY

A leader with a jealous heart cannot inspire. Inspiration requires that the leader give and give freely without expectations. Jealousy will get in the way of inspiring others.

PREACHING

Inspiring isn't about preaching. Just as most teenagers tune out preachy messages, so do most adults. When the leader tells people what they *should* do and why they *should* do it, that's not inspiration, it's telling. The inspiring leader helps people recognize and come to their own conclusions.

JUDGING OR CRITICIZING

Another sure way to kill emerging inspiration is to judge or criticize. Judging or criticizing usually turns people into defensive, protective creatures rather than open and growing beings.

Cathy walked into her new job feeling confident and happy. This job was the opportunity she had been waiting for. With 20 years of experience, she felt prepared and skilled to face the challenges in this new position. Then, she met Dick.

At 8:15 A.M., the first words she heard from Dick were, "I expected you to be here earlier." Feeling embarrassed, she apologized. The people in human resources had told her to report at 8:30 A.M. She didn't bother to explain that to Dick because she didn't want to sound defensive.

The next day, she and Dick attended a meeting. Cathy had lots of experience on the subject, so after listening intently, she offered some ideas to the group. After the meeting, Dick told Cathy that she shouldn't offer her opinion until she knows what she's talking about.

Week after week, Dick had something critical to say. At first, Cathy apologized and tried to learn what Dick wanted. After a while, her enthusiasm turned into doubt. Maybe she couldn't do this job. Maybe she wasn't good enough. But she kept trying.

And so did Dick. He tried — successfully — to find things to criticize. Cathy's presentation skills were one of her greatest gifts. However, after each presentation, Dick would find something about it he didn't like. Now, the voice of doubt nagged more loudly at Cathy. She found herself focusing less and less on trying and more and more on hiding.

Then, of course, Dick criticized her for inaction. Eight months after walking enthusiastically in the door, Cathy now walked out each day in defeat. In desperation one evening, she considered downing a bottle of sleeping pills. At that moment, she realized how much damage Dick had inflicted.

If a leader could have that much influence to cause such a downward spiral, imagine, if that same power were used to create upward spirals. Those upward spirals, complete with instilling confidence, self-esteem, and renewal are the essence of inspiration.

LETTER TO LEADERS

To the leaders of the world,

   You've been called to walk a special
path. It is a path filled with
uncomfortable deadlines, tense moments,
difficult decisions, and certain uncertainty.

   You may build bridges or buildings
or widgets. But don't lose sight of the
fact that, most definitely, leading is
about building people's spirits. The
path you've chosen has placed you in a
position to touch these spirits in a
way that others cannot.

   Along the way, you will encounter
much ugliness. You will see the human
spirit at its worst. Pettiness and
jealousy, rage and cowardice will
present themselves--in your followers,
and perhaps in you. When you encounter
this side, in a moment of despair, you
will wonder if leadership is worth the
struggle. You may be tempted to give up
the fight--to find a new path.

   Ultimately, you will decide to stay
on this path, or to leave it for
another. If you choose to stay, I hope
you do so with a certain dream in your
heart--the dream of inspiring people.

But there is mystery in inspiring. And hopefully, this mystery will remain. The leader's job is not to understand this mystery. It is only to act as a conduit for it. As you strive to unlock the human potential within your workplace, your journey as leader begins. As you become more skilled, you come closer to helping people reach their inspiration points and find true meaning in their work and joy in the workplace. In the process, you become selfless and serve a Source higher than your boss or your company. As you dance with this Higher Source and teach others to do the same, then you become a leader.

As you turn on the music in the souls of others, you will find the music in your own soul grows sweeter. Your company, your followers, and you will find new meaning and new profits-- both measurable and immeasurable.

Have a wonderful life,

Adele B. Lynn

APPENDIX —
THE STAFF MEETING

AGENDA

Step 1 — Face the Problem

Step 2 — Commit to Change

Step 3 — Analyze the Present

Step 4 — Zero In on the Significant Few

Step 5 — Select Values Carefully

Step 6 — Remember What Works

Step 7 — Install a Guidance System

Step 8 — Deal with the Exceptions in a Fair and
Equitable Manner

Step 9 — Celebrate Successes

AGENDA: *Step 1 — Face the Problem*

"We have to do something, Joe. We can't just sit back and say, 'Well, that's just the way it is here. It has always been this way.' We are the leaders of this organization," Harry said. "It is our responsibility to change things." His face was turning crimson as it did when he got angry.

"That's fine Harry, but it just doesn't work," Joe said. "We've tried some things before. We have had a string of consultants in here, and they all told us that we have a very strong culture at this plant. People have been conditioned not to put forth much effort. Besides, our union is very powerful. You can't just expect those things to go away." Joe's answer implied that Harry should have been paying attention for the past five years.

June spoke up and added her frustrations to the heap. "I am responsible for getting product out the door. I can't take valuable time out of my day to debate such matters. I have enough to worry about without talking about things that never seem to change anyway."

"Besides," Joel chimed in, "instead of sitting here wasting time, we should be out there watching to make sure they are working. They are probably on a 45-minute coffee break as we speak."

Ned had been listening to this verbal brouhaha for about 10 minutes and decided it was high time for getting his jabs in, too. "Look at us. This kind of stuff gives our people the liberty to do anything they want. They know that we can't or won't do anything about our problems because we can't agree as a management team."

This entire discussion had captured Catherine's attention. She listened intently to each person. Although Catherine had been at the plant for only about three months, she had a long and respected career within the division. There was something about her that was hard to describe. She didn't come across as arrogant or preachy; she just seemed to have a sense of understanding that was deeper than most people's. She realized the company had to improve the way it worked with its people, but she also knew she had encountered many good people at the plant who seemed to care about their work. Finally, with what seemed to be impeccable timing, calmly and confidently, she announced, "I think each of you is right."

Perhaps the group was just tired of the bickering, or perhaps they all needed some confirmation. Whatever the reason, everyone stopped and listened to Catherine.

"Joe is correct in his assessment. The problems within our organization have been present for a long time, and they aren't going to go away overnight. And, yes, I can appreciate your concerns, June, regarding getting product out the door. It does seem like a waste of time to just sit and talk about the problems, doesn't it, Joel? And Ned, we don't seem to be able to agree on what to do about it yet. As Harry said, we are the leaders." Catherine said in summary.

"So, great," Joe said. "We are all correct. That doesn't get us any closer to changing anything, does it?"

"I think it does." Catherine said. " I think we can come up with a plan."

"But before we do, let's do some homework," she said. "Let's get some information. I think it's important that we come to agreement that we really do have a problem."

In order to face the problem, we have to ask the tough questions.

1. Do people feel a sense of importance regarding their job? Do employees think management believes what they do is important? Do employees believe that management values them as individuals?

2. Are people concerned about the well-being of others in the workplace? Do employees believe that management cares about them? Does management show their concern about the whole person? Does management show an interest in people?

3. Do people feel that management sincerely appreciates their effort? Are appreciation and reward programs met with skepticism?

4. Are people feeling resentment, inequity, or a sense of unfairness over workplace contributions? The following comments reveal the symptom:

EMPLOYEES ABOUT MANAGEMENT:

❖ All they do is sit in meetings. They don't even know what we do.

❖ When we have a problem, my supervisor walks away. He doesn't care. He just tells me to solve it. What the hell do I have a supervisor for?

❖ Management just takes care of themselves. They don't care about us.

❖ They expect us to do all the work while they go golfing.

❖ All they ever do is push for more and more from us. Yet, they never lift a finger. They just point them.

MANAGEMENT ABOUT EMPLOYEES:

❖ If we're not out there watching over things, nothing gets done.

❖ Why do I have to solve all of their problems?

❖ We're paying them to think. Why don't they start doing it?

❖ We're not paying people to sit around. We're paying them to work. We're tired of their nonchalant attitudes.

❖ There is no sense of urgency with our employees. All of the burden is on management.

EMPLOYEES ABOUT CO-WORKERS:

- ❖ I'm not going to bust my butt. Susie doesn't do anything, and no one says anything to her.

- ❖ Why does he get all the perks? He started after me.

- ❖ I hear Johnny gets to go to another seminar. When's it my turn?

- ❖ Susie got another easy job. I have a project that will take the rest of my life.

- ❖ Well, Kim's in the boss's office again. Wonder what she's sucking up for now?

CAUTION: Every person in every workplace thinks these things sometimes. What we're looking for here is whether or not this is a typical description of the perceptions in your workplace. If so, face the problem.

5. Are people working toward the same vision? Are your teams aligned? Are they pulling in one direction? Do they believe in the same thing? Do they work toward the same goals? Which column better describes your team?

CAUTION: Even the best high-performance teams may occasionally display behaviors that are misaligned. How do your teams normally function? If they normally function as described in the right-hand column, face the problem.

Teams Aligned	Teams Not Aligned
High energy	Lethargic
See work as exciting	See work as a chore
Enthusiasm for assignments	No enthusiasm for assignments
Quick turnaround	Slow response
Open	Cautious, suspicious
Creative	Stuck
United	Splintered and fractious
Will move issues forward conclusion	Will stall or delay issues to with debate, further study, or other means
Will openly offer opinions	Will only state opinions in safety of small factions
Respect	Quiet or open contempt
Conflict with open discussion and resolution	Conflict with no resolution, Stalemate
Win–Win	Win–Lose
Disagreement on Issues	Disagreement on Values
Shares credit and highlights others	Competitive, jealous, and skeptical of achievements of others

AGENDA: *Step 2 — Commit to Change*

"This is really tough," Ned said. "It's one thing to complain in a staff meeting every now and then, but now, we actually have to face it. We do have a problem."

"I wish we hadn't even brought this up," Joe said, face in his hands. "It would be easier just to forget it."

"You know, we'd just be kidding ourselves though," Harry said. "These problems exist whether we admit it or not."

June jumped in. "Yes, but to admit that we don't trust our employees, they don't trust us, and we aren't functioning very well, that we aren't aligned to one vision, it just makes me feel like I've failed."

Catherine nodded and smiled a bit. "Leadership is hard work," she said. "The real failure comes if we don't address it. It takes courage to face the facts."

"Yeah, but now what," Joel asked?

"Well," Ned asked, "do we want to try to fix it or not?"

"We don't even know what to fix or how," Joe said. "I don't know. Maybe we should leave well enough alone. Besides, we may do more harm than good."

"Oh, come on." Harry said, shifting in his chair. "How can we not do something about this? This isn't going to get better by putting our heads in the sand or wishing it away."

June shook her head. "Yeah, I know," she said, "but

this isn't going to be fixed overnight. Besides, with the pressures of getting product out the door, do we have the time to undertake something this big?"

"Do you think it's going to go away if we ignore it?" Harry persisted.

"Look," Ned answered, "if we're committed to trying to change this culture, I think we have to realize that we could be looking at a two- to five-year plan, and that may be optimistic. Besides, I would like to get a retirement check from this place. If we continue at this rate, I might not have that opportunity. I say we have to."

"I think it's the right thing to do," Harry said.

"Me too," Joel said.

"I dunno," Joe said. "I'm skeptical."

Catherine wanted consensus. "What would help you change your mind?" she asked.

"If I could see this work somewhere," Joe said. "If I knew what we were planning to do. If I knew what we wanted to become. Right now it just seems so fuzzy."

"I know a company that was in worse shape than ours," Catherine said. "Let's plan a visit."

One week later...

"Well, that was impressive," Joe conceded. "I guess I'm ready to say yes. I'm still worried that this isn't going to be easy... .

"It isn't," Harry interrupted. "But that's why they pay us the big bucks, right? Where do we start?"

AGENDA: *Step 3 – Analyze the Present*

"Well, let's see," Harry said. "They said it's important to analyze the present. They said something about analyzing five levels."

"Yes, let's see," June said, flipping through a tablet. "I wrote them down. 'The five levels of contribution in the workplace are: tasks, roles, behaviors, performance, and values.'

"They said that problems can occur on any of these five levels." she said. "They said that often, we don't realize we actually are reinforcing things that are counter to what we want to accomplish."

"Yes," Ned said. "I think they said the watchwords were actions and reactions to all five levels."

"Let's see," Harry said, "how would we ... ."

Let's look at contributions in the workplace on five different levels. **These five levels are tasks, roles, behaviors, performance, and values.** Analyze the messages you send to your staff each day on these five levels

TASKS

Leader discusses: *What needs to be done?*

Leader considers: *Experience and training level of the employees*
Respect for the employee's knowledge and skill
People's need for freedom of action

Over the next couple of weeks, analyze each uncompleted or under- completed task. Some things we take for granted are under-completed tasks. Look at all aspects of the task: quality, cost, and time.

Does the supervisor routinely include employees in identifying the tasks and the how-tos?

Should the supervisor have given a more detailed explanation?

Should the employee have asked for clarification?

Should the supervisor have asked more questions?

Did the employee know what was expected?

Should they have known?

How should they have known?

What mechanisms are in place for people to know what is expected?

However, equally important, if not more so, are the reactions to unmet expectations. Whatever reaction we have to those unmet expectations send still more messages to employees. For each uncompleted or under-completed task, ask the following:

Should management have disciplined or even fired the employee?

Should management have disciplined or even fired the supervisor?

Even though the result wasn't accomplished, what did the employee do right in this incident? Did the employee think independently? Did he show concern for product quality? Production time?

What did management do right?

What actions, behaviors, or values were reinforced by management's actions or inactions?

Each of these reactions sends different underlying messages that affect the culture and set expectations for the next situation. The leader's behavior, both in setting expectations and in reacting to situations, sends strong messages to the staff. Employees interpret these messages and draw conclusions about their contributions and the contributions of management. What logical conclusions do employees draw from your actions or reactions related to tasks in the workplace? Think about it.

ROLES
> **Leader discusses:** *Who should do what?*
>
> **Leader considers:** *Experience and training level of the employees. Which job function is best suited to get the task done? Special gifts, strengths, and interests of the team members.*

A boss attached a note explaining where to file each piece of paper that passed through her desk, yet complained that her secretary couldn't come up with a filing system of her own. When I talked to the secretary about this, she clearly did not think her boss expected her to come up with a system. Wonder why?

Analyze the work unit: Who does what? Who should be doing what? Use flow charts to diagram present tasks and responsibilities. Involve employees in the analysis. **Ask employees for their opinions for improvement.**

Does the supervisor, when appropriate, consult employees in determining roles?

Has the supervisor analyzed the work flow?

Has the supervisor, when appropriate, asked for volunteers for certain jobs?

BEHAVIORS

> **Leader discusses:** *How things get done, in what demeanor and with what behaviors or attitudes.*

> **Leader considers:** *Experience and training level of the employees.*

What behaviors or attitudes will produce the best business result?
What do internal and external customers want?
What do your employees think are appropriate and inappropriate behaviors?
What behaviors do you reward in the workplace?
What behaviors are unacceptable?
What behaviors should be unacceptable, yet are condoned?

PERFORMANCE

> **Leader discusses:** *What is an acceptable level of job performance. It measures the quantity and quality of task performance.*

> **Leader considers:** *Experience and training level of the employees.*

What performance level will produce the best business result?
What do internal and external customers want?
At a manufacturing plant that produces molded plastic containers, material is cycled through many different pieces of equipment in order to produce the final product. Four minutes in machine A, three minutes in machine B, nine minutes in machine C. Barring any machine difficulties or material problems, the whole process is predictable. Management knows that an experienced operator can produce a certain number of pieces per hour. Yet, let's assume that a few

operators decided not to trouble themselves to make the numbers. What do you suppose could happen if management turns its back to these few operators and ignores the problem?

Have employees been involved in setting standards?
What are the standards at the workplace?
Are people aware of the standards?
What happens if standards are met?
What happens if standards are not met?
What standards are valued or devalued?

VALUES

Leader discusses: *Why we do what we do in the way that we do it. It constitutes the foundation of our corporate belief system.*

Leader considers: *What values will produce the best business result?*

If management says it values quality, then puts on the market a product that has a known defect, it shows employees that management doesn't value quality. If management says it values customer service, then argues with customers about their problems, it doesn't value customer service. If the written values statement says management communicates openly and honestly, then debates whether or not to share information with employees, it doesn't value open communications.

These inconsistent values messages provide ample opportunity for the organizational cynics and comics. They provide ripe ground for breeding discontent and distrust.

What do employees value? What should they value?

When does management mouth one value and live another?
Which values are sacred in the workplace?
What should be valued in the workplace?
What values are in place that jeopardize the business goals?

We believe the four core trust values proposed in this book — importance, touch, gratitude, and fair and equal contributions — are important to every workplace. Therefore, we recommend that leaders strongly consider including these core values when determining the appropriate business values for their organization.

AGENDA: *Step 4 — Zero In on the Significant Few*

"I had no idea we were making so many mistakes," June said.

"Yeah, this is depressing," Ned agreed. "We're messing up on all five levels. I want to change everything."

"Oh, come on," Harry said. "We're not that bad. We've identified some things we do right. Yeah, we learned that one thing we do right all the time is getting the shipment out on time. No matter what."

"We also found out that we really do value safety at this plant," Joe observed. "This is an area where we don't compromise."

"Yeah," Joel said, "it's one area where our people respect us."

"I think," Catherine said, "the key is to zero in on a few important things on each of the five levels that we want to change."

Joe looked at her. "What were those steps to change...?

FIVE LEVELS — FIVE STEPS

1. Invite people into discussion and dialogue about what is important on all five levels. Engage their thoughts and their hearts in changing things for the better.

2. Always answer this question: What is the goal for each level?

   For example, what is the goal regarding tasks? For employees to take ownership of the tasks?

3. Select the "Significant Few" for each level. Concentrate on changing just a few things at a time. Everyone's attention should be on these few items.

4. Empower employees to reach the "Significant Few."

5. Together with employees, monitor, evaluate, and continuously improve on all five levels. Link rewards and systems to support the goals.

AGENDA: *Step 5 — Select Values Carefully*

"What about values?" Joe wanted to know. "That seems like a tough one. I'm not sure how to approach that. Besides, do we really have a right to mess with people's values?"

"We're not talking about personal values, here," Harry explained. "We're talking about business values. The values that are necessary to help us achieve our business goals. Values like quality, respect for each other's opinions, and safety. We don't care if people vote Democrat or Republican."

"How do we even begin a discussion around values?" June asked.

VALUES

Values are the toughest and the most important issue for leaders to address. Values can have a powerful impact on what people do every day in the workplace. Although clear expectations are important at all levels and will help people do the right things, probably the most significant influence in determining our actions are our values — both our personal values and the group values.

The first step is to define the shared values that are acceptable from a business point of view. This can be done by meeting with workers and defining values and examples of behaviors that reflect each value, as well as examples of behaviors that erode each value. The goal at this step isn't to try to define each and every possible behavior.

Instead, these discussions serve as a way to further the understanding and definition of each value.

The following template can be used for this purpose:

VALUES	BEHAVIOR	ANTI-BEHAVIOR
"I believe in..."	"therefore, I will..."	"therefore, I will not..."
Example: I believe in showing respect for others in the workplace,	1. therefore, I will listen actively when people state their opinions. 2. therefore, I will greet people when I walk in their presence. 3. therefore, I will seek opinions of all my teammates.	1. therefore, I will not ridicule or criticize opinions I disagree with. 2. therefore, I will not direct profanity at people. 3. therefore, I will not embarrass people by pointing out mistakes in front of others. 4. therefore, I will not belittle a person's idea to another person.

The values template serves as a way to dialogue with employees around values. Trim the list to a manageable few that will help deliver the business goals. This will help employees and management have a common understanding of the shared values that are important to the business. These shared values serve the team as the rules or standards of conduct that members are expected to follow. As long as the members demonstrate these shared values, they are included and valued within the group. They serve as fuel for the group or team to accomplish tasks or missions. If the values are aligned within the group, the power and energy are high. If the values are not aligned, the fuel is low.

AGENDA: *Step 6 — Remember What Works*

"...That took some work, but I think we have identified our shared business values and expectations," Catherine said. "I especially like the list of behaviors that help us recognize when we are in sync with the values and when we are not. Well, what do you think?"

"I don't know, Catherine, this may have been good for us to clarify what is important to us, but I just don't think this is going to make any difference. I've participated in these kinds of things in the past. My experience tells me that these things just get stuck in a drawer somewhere. No one really pays attention to these kinds of things after the meeting. I remember the last company I worked for had a great list of values that we developed at a weekend retreat, but everyday reality was so far from that list. Besides, we still have the pressures of production." Joe continued to list his concerns. "I'm not trying to be negative, but I am trying to be a realist."

"Joe's right, just because we have a list of clear expectations and business values doesn't necessarily change anything. So everyone knows what they are supposed to contribute, how do we go about really changing things?" Ned asked trying to hold back the skepticism.

"Catherine, I can see how if everyone lived these values, this organization would be a better place, but I just can't see how this changes anything. I still have the same people every day and the same product every day to get out the door. Frankly, I'm concerned that it will be business as usual." June echoed.

Catherine listened intently as the group commented. "Well, again, you are all right. These values and expectations won't serve us well if we keep them in the drawer. And nothing will change without a great deal of effort on our part and indeed it will be business as usual. But I think we can make this happen. Let's draw on our experience and list what we already know about making expectations stick. People contribute when..."

PEOPLE CONTRIBUTE WHEN THE EXPECTATIONS ARE:	
CLEAR	Clearly understood expectations help take the confusion away for people. Clearly understood means that people have an opportunity to ask questions, respond to, and otherwise do what it takes to understand the expectation. It does not imply that the leader must "tell" people what to do. Communication is a two-way process that invites both parties to come to understanding regarding the issue.
CONSISTENT	The surest way to see to it that expectations don't take hold within a culture is to be inconsistent or selective about applying the expectation. Sure, there may be exceptions, but for the most part, leaders must clearly define the expectations, then any exception should have a clear reason that rational people would be able to understand.
RESPECTFUL OF OTHER PARTY	The manner in which expectations are communicated should demonstrate respect for individuals. However, beyond communication, the expectations themselves should also show respect for others. What is a reasonable expectation to have regarding work habits, hours, workplace values etc.? Would most people in the

	workplace consider these expectations reasonable? Does the expectation make sense? Is there a good reason for the expectation? Is the expectation based on a business need or the preferences of a particular leader?
SUPPORTED BY ALL MEMBERS OF THE LEADERSHIP TEAM	If a leader intends to establish an expectation for a good business reason, it must be supported by all members of the leader's team. Of course, the best way to enlist the support of all members of the group is to include them in defining what the expectations should be.

AGENDA: *Step 7 — Install a Guidance System*

"But we have always known these things, Catherine. That hasn't helped us in the past." Joe's frustration was back. "I just don't think things will ever change."

"It is true, we are our own worst enemy. It's even worse when we know that we are the problem." said Ned.

"Yeah, and like I've been saying, my production load isn't going to change. The daily routine just dictates what I can do and what I can't do." June said in a resigned tone.

" I don't think so," Catherine calmly reassured the group. " I think we can use this information to help us watch out so we don't repeat our mistakes."

"Do we all agree that our actions or inactions at least in part influence the expectations?" Catherine asked.

" Well yeah, but.... "

"Then I'm suggesting that we start there. We may not be able to change everything, but we can work to change the messages that we give. Isn't that right?" Catherine asked.

"How would we do that?" Joe said. "As we said, this information isn't new and unfortunately, it hasn't changed anything so far." Joe continued.

"Well, do you think we could come up with some kind of a support system that could help us?" Catherine asked. "Kind of like a mirror that will let us know if we are on track."

" You mean like a guidance system on an aircraft? Hmm, well maybe if...." said Harry.

Sometimes, we're so clever we can mess up without even knowing. Every leader needs information that enables her to know if she is on the correct course. Likewise, if headed off course, some type of feedback system is also essential. Two guidance systems can be used to provide such feedback to the leader(s).

CORPORATE SOUL KEEPERS (VALUES GROUP)

A group of individuals within the organization can help the leader understand how the corporate values are being internalized at various levels of the organization. This group would work with the leader to monitor the agreed-upon corporate values. They would compare reality and the stated values and point out inconsistencies between the two. These corporate soul keepers will help the leader understand what actions are upholding the corporate values and what actions are eroding the stated values. For example, if a shared value is to respect other employees, and the group knows that members of management routinely belittle employees, criticize employee in front of others, use foul language when referring to employees, or otherwise demonstrate disrespectful behaviors, then the leader must be told about these inconsistencies. By preserving the corporate values and expectations, the leader can bring about the type of culture that is conducive to success.

It is important that this group of corporate soul keepers isn't set up as a watchdog group, but rather as a mirror for the leader. This is a feedback mechanism for the leader. The function of this group isn't to go out and tell others that they are not upholding the corporate values. It is also not a tattletale group that gives specific names and incidents to the leader. Instead, it helps the leader understand and then educate others on how the corporate values are being interpreted through everyday actions.

The size of the group should be five to nine members and criteria for members would include the following:

a) a willingness to communicate concerns openly

b) a willingness to speak the truth when they believe that the values of the group are at risk

c) an open-minded, broad view that can see beyond a personal perspective

d) perceived by others as having the above three criteria

This group would meet regularly with the leader in roundtable format to discuss the shared values and to discuss concerns, progress, and perspective regarding the identified values. The feedback from this group would be aimed at the organization in general, not at a specific individual. This group would also look at aspects of the organization — such as reward systems, communications, training, performance systems, and structure — that would link and reinforce the desired values throughout the entire culture.

REVERSE MENTORING

Mentoring has long been used as a way for individuals to gain insight about their behaviors and as a forum for growth and development. The traditional context of mentoring typically sets up a senior person in rank or status with a junior person. However, if we depart from the traditional approach and set up reverse mentoring relationships, the leaders can grow as an integral part of the team rather than the traditional hierarchical authority. The purpose of reverse mentoring relationships would be to give senior rank leaders information that will allow them to understand the impact and perception of their behavior in the context of the shared values.

The reverse mentoring would help individual leaders understand how their behavior is perceived. Mentoring will tell the leader which of the behaviors reinforces the values and which weaken or diminish the shared value structure. Reverse mentoring should give individual leaders specific information regarding their behavior as leaders, whereas, the values group is designed to give overall feedback regarding the general progress and direction of the organization related to its values.

Reverse mentoring relationships should be established with the following in mind:

a) The mentees should be leaders within the organization who are willing to receive honest information regarding the perceptions of their behaviors within the organization

b) The mentors should be people within the organization who are respected by the mentee as well as others within the organization

c) The mentors and mentees should participate voluntarily

d) The mentors and mentees should agree to be paired with their respective partner

e) The mentors and mentees should understand the shared values that the organization has agreed to

Some companies, when implementing the Corporate Soul Keepers group and the Reverse Mentoring, have kept the identity of the group members and mentors confidential at first. Ideally, this should flow in an open and unrestricted way; however, some cultures would not permit this kind of exchange initially. The benefit of starting Soul Keepers and Reverse Mentoring anonymously outweighed the drawbacks of anonymity.

AGENDA: *Step 8 — Deal with the Exceptions in a Fair and Equitable Manner*

"These systems might sound OK when we talk about them, but, frankly, they make me kind of nervous," said June. "There are some people out there who just don't like

me, and I guess I just don't want to see this turn into some
kind of personal attack."

"Yeah, June's right. We get on their backs about production, and they report us to this Soul Committee," Joel
chimed in kind of nervously.

"Besides, how much time would this take away from
the job?" June asked.

In a surprise change of heart, Joe responded, "You
know, June, you do have a tough job, so I can understand
why you might be concerned. Frankly, this makes me nervous too. But I really am tired of living with the same
problems for so many years. It seems like we just complain
about them but they never go away. And I'm actually one
of the biggest complainers. So I think we should go ahead
with this, but I also think we need to make a pact between
us that we do this in the right spirit. We aren't doing this
to hurt anyone. We're doing it to help all of us set the
example to lead us to a better place."

"You know, I think Joe said something that we all
need to take to heart. We need to do this in the right
spirit," said Harry.

"Well, I'm nervous, too, but I'm game, and I'll be sure
to remind us if we somehow stray from doing this with the
right intentions or spirit," Ned said half jokingly and half
serious.

"Actually, I think that's an important part of this. We
need to check in with each other to make sure that every-

one is OK. Remember, we are doing this to improve the overall values in the workplace, so we don't want to do harm along the way," said Joel.

"Yeah," Harry said. "I think this will work if we all keep the right perspective, but I also believe that we can't really learn anything or change unless we feel some pain. I think there may be some unpleasant feedback coming our way. After all, the culture is this way in part because of what we have done or not done."

"True," Ned said, "I think this could get uncomfortable. But we are the leaders here. If we ever want to make a difference, I think this is our opportunity."

"Are we all in agreement?" Catherine asked. They all said they were. "Then let's move forward," she said.

"The Corporate Soul Group and the Reverse Mentoring will help us do the right things," June cautioned, "but what do we do if our employees aren't meeting our expectations?"

Somewhere along this path, the leader will encounter this challenge. Some people will not accept the changes. At this point, the leader's role is to coach with touch to help the employee to make the transition and go along with the change.

However, a few people may not respond to the coaching. At this point, the leader must face the truth with a gentle heart. Yes, leaders can and must use touch even when they fire people.

AGENDA: *Step 9 — Celebrate Successes*

"It's been a long haul," Catherine observed, "but we made it."

"Yeah," Joe said. "Do you remember two years ago when we sat around and complained about how bad it was?"

"You were the biggest complainer, too," Harry teased. "You were our biggest skeptic."

"Frankly, I used to get really annoyed with you. But you know, if it wasn't for your complaining all the time, we probably wouldn't have done anything."

"Our people really came through," June said. "I know we still have a few problems, but, it's so different than it was before."

"You know, you can see it in their faces," Ned said. "People are happier. I think they really expected us to do something about the way things were."

"You know, you're right," Joe said. "Just the other day, Janie in IMS told me that two years ago she was getting her resume updated. Now, she says she doesn't even look at the want ads."

"Jim said that he hated to come to work," Joel added. "Now, he actually looks forward to it. He said even his wife was amazed."

"Did you hear what our union president had to say?" Harry asked.

"What?" Joe asked.

Harry looked all around the table. "He said he didn't think we had it in us. He said he didn't think we would stick to it. He said that at first all he heard were words, never assumed we would really change and expect people to change. It was quite a compliment from him."

"Where is he anyway?" June asked.

"I'm here," he said walking through the door, "and I heard that! Don't let it go to your head. You can't quit now or we'll be right back where we started."

"That's true," Catherine said, "but we can stop and celebrate how far we've come.

"Yeah, let's get on with it," Joel agreed.

"We need to make sure this celebration includes everyone," Ned said. "Let's put some teams together of our employees to help us plan."

"I want to be on the entertainment team," the union president said. "I'm looking forward to having a management roast. I know I could get volunteers for that one."

SEMINARS, WORKSHOPS, AND KEYNOTE PRESENTATIONS
AIMED AT BUILDING HONOR ARE AVAILABLE FOR YOUR
ORGANIZATION.

FOR MORE INFORMATION CONTACT:

ADELE B. LYNN
LYNN LEARNING LABS
609 BROAD AVE.
BELLE VERNON, PA   15012

724 929-5352

EMAIL: LYNNLABS@WESTOL.COM
WWW.LYNNLEARNINGLABS.COM

ACKNOWLEDGMENTS

Hundreds of people have shaped the ideas presented on the pages of this book. My special thanks to all the people in the workplace who spoke openly and candidly in order to make the world of work a better place - a place of honor. Without them, there would be no story to tell. Special thanks to my many clients who gave me permission to get close enough to tell the story.

I also heartily acknowledge three people whose support and expert guidance contributed greatly to the final product. Special thanks to Earl McDaniel, my editor, who slaved over pages and pages of manuscript. His insistence on word pictures shows on every page. Donna Kuhl, whose constant faith in the importance of this work and my ability to carry this message inspired me to finish what I had started. Our bottomless conversations show up everywhere on the pages of this book. Thanks also to Hal Swart, who spent countless hours explaining the obvious to me. I think I got it now.

Special thanks to Jeff Herman, literary agent, who believed in this work when it was an untitled manuscript and I most needed a professional to say "yes."

I appreciated the contributions of Coletta Perry and Debra Propes, whose artful way with type and graphics, made me proud of the physical appearance of this book. Diane Hartman thanks for your careful eyes.

Bill, thanks for the space, patience, and love. Thank you Janele, for enduring "the book." No one had to listen to my endless babble about this project more than the two of you. Mom and Dad, thank you for teaching me the basics about honor. Karl, thanks for your kinship turned friendship.

I am most grateful to God for the Divine guidance received throughout this project and throughout my life.